"A must read"

"Successful companies in the 21st century will be those that build their strategies based on the interdependence of their economic, environmental and social risks, opportunities and performance. The insights in this book are based on Bruce's intense curiosity about the world and business and makes this book a must read."

–Gord Lambert
President, GRL Collaboration

"Clear and important"

"Over the years, Bruce Piasecki's workshops have drawn in numerous business leaders from some of the world's top firms. He has been an alert chronicler here. *New World Companies* distills some of the most critical aspects of future growth and investment strategies into clear and important advice."

–Dennis Welch
EVP and Chief External Officer
American Electric Power

"Smart investing"

"Socially responsive or sustainable investing is an exploding sector of the investment universe. . . . Bruce Piasecki's *New World Companies* clearly explains how such investing is "smart investing" and also reflects the growing understanding that being a responsible corporation is good business."

–Timothy Smith
Director, ESG Shareowner Engagement
Walden Asset Management

OTHER TITLES BY BRUCE PIASECKI

NEW WORLD COMPANIES

THE FUTURE OF CAPITALISM

BRUCE PIASECKI

SQUAREONE
PUBLISHERS

COVER DESIGNER: Jeannie Tudor
IN-HOUSE EDITOR: Marie Caratozzolo
TYPESETTER: Gary A. Rosenberg

Square One Publishers
115 Herricks Road
Garden City Park, NY 11040
(516) 535-2010 • (877) 900-BOOK
www.squareonepublishers.com

Library of Congress Cataloging-in-Publication Data

Name: Piasecki, Bruce, 1955- author.
Title: New world companies : the future of capitalism / Bruce Piasecki.
Description: Garden City Park, NY : Square One Publishers, [2016] | Includes
    bibliographical references and index.
Identifiers: LCCN 2015035680 | ISBN 9780757004131 (paper) ISBN
    9780757054136 (ebook)
Subjects: LCSH: International business enterprises. | Social responsibility of
    business. | Technological innovations—Economic aspects. | Sustainable
    development.
Classification: LCC HD2755.5 .P5623 2016 | DDC 338.8/8—dc23
LC record available at http://lccn.loc.gov/2015035680

Printed in the United States of America

10   9   8   7   6   5   4   3   2

Contents

Credits

The image in Figure 2.1 "Practical Sustainability" (page 47) is provided by FedEx.

The images in Figure 2.2 "Increasing Focus on Climate Risk" (page 54) and Figure 2.3 "Projected Costs of Restricting CO_2 Emissions" (page 55) are provided by ExxonMobil Corporation.

"The Iceberg Balance Sheet" in Figure 4.1 (page 100) is provided by Innovest.

The graphics in Figure 6.1 "The Hybrid Powertrain Factor" (page 138) and Figure 6.3 "Toyota's Sustainability Focus" (page 144) are provided by Toyota.

Acknowledgments

This book would not have been possible without the rich contributions of a number of people who have supported me both personally and professionally.

Up front, my thanks to Marti Simmons, who organizes my travels, my firm, our staff, our clients, our workshops, and our corporate affiliates. Without Marti, I would not know where I stand some weeks.

During the six years of writing this book, I have had the pleasure and privilege of meeting with many of the business leaders and gifted executives representing a number of today's new world companies—including such corporate giants as Suncor, FedEx, Exxon-Mobil, Caterpillar, Siemens, Flex, and Toyota, to name just a few. These industry experts have shared insights and information that have been integral additions to this book. I truly appreciate you and all that you have contributed.

I must also offer my sincere gratitude to the sustained efforts of a very special group of people working within my firm. From weekly group talks with our senior associates to our relentless researchers and office colleagues—such as Stephen Gardner of Los Angeles; Evan Forward of Burlington, Vermont; Michael Spanos of Athens, Greece; Sebastian Vanderzeil of Manhattan and Northern Australia; Selena Griffith of Sydney, Australia; and Mike Sharpe at our headquarters in

Saratoga, New York. Thank you for your thoughts, contributions, and influences—all of which are reflected in this text.

In my first four decades as a business professional, I was listening to a kind of internal standard, making my way, finding my voice and signature—before I could conceive an integrative book like this one. This time-released realization brings me full circle to another formidable mentor and friend I must acknowledge. For the basic faith that this studied history-based approach pays off, I thank my initial PhD chairman at Cornell, the legendary M. H. Abrams—author of such works as *The Norton Anthology of English Literature* and *Glossary of Literary Terms.* I am deeply grateful to this man for his rigorous and mindful training. He inspired me, indirectly, to leave pre-med training and step into the ever-evolving and emotionally rich and moving world of literary and cultural history. He changed both the course and the intensity of my life.

Also included in this book are the fingerprints of those who demand good writing and logical thinking. They include my wife, Andrea Carol Masters, my college friend Sandy Chizinsky, attorney Michael Libonati, and my former editor Peter Lynch. Special thanks to my publisher and founder of Square One, Rudy Shur—now the force behind four of my books. I would also like to acknowledge his devoted and talented editor Marie Caratozzolo.

My wife once said, "Bruce, tact is the intelligence of the soul." I would have been left behind, tactless, were it not for this red-headed kid whom I first encountered nearly four decades ago. Here also is my thanks to our daughter, Colette, for her strength and her steady faith in Dad, who travels widely and too much.

In the words of Helen Keller: "Walking with a friend in the dark is better than walking alone in the light." With friends like Rudy Shur, Andrea Carol Masters, Marie Caratozzolo, Peter Lynch, Sandy Chizinsky, and M. H. Abrams, I have been able, in this short life, to enjoy more light than dark.

Foreword

The human imagination has always been captivated by the notion of giants roaming the earth. Today, giants *do* roam the earth—we call them corporations.

In *New World Companies*, Bruce Piasecki dramatically evaluates the social capital these giants yield. He shows how firms are competing now and will continue to compete in the future regarding money, people, and rules. Piasecki gives us reasons to hope that the universal social urgencies surrounding these companies—such as environmental degradation, poverty, climate change, population growth, access to education, and raw material resourcefulness—will make them compete in new and more innovative ways. He suggests astute ways to get within the walls of these firms to understand what makes them tick. In short, Piasecki gives us a reliable glimpse of our shared future with these new world companies, while providing us with a witty, illustrated, and colorful account of social history.

Why has he done this, and why now?

For better or worse, corporations are among the most powerful and influential entities on the planet. In 2012, of the world's 100 largest financial entities, 40 percent were corporations. Expanding that number from 100 to 150, nearly 60 percent were corporations. If Facebook were a country, it would be the most populous nation on earth, as the huge social network claims that 1.39 billion people log onto its site each month. In our interconnected world, the way in which corporations manage their operations has a profound effect on virtually everyone on the planet.

New World Companies is a straightforward and eye-opening view of the "modern"—the essence of our time—that pertains to all investors, business leaders, and social activists. The insights it offers to our growing interconnected world prove exceptional and useful, offering a hopeful future in which the pressing social needs of our world can be answered. This book illustrates how corporate strategy takes into account all three dimensions of sustainable development (people, planet, economic growth) in a balanced and profitable manner, going beyond the traditional management practices taught in school. It is a reflection of Piasecki's entire career, which has been devoted to promoting forms of innovation and the themes of this book.

There is still a bigger surprise in this book before you.

Piasecki then pictures the future of capitalism, which some call *sustainable capitalism*. The engagement of financial-services conglomerates into the ESG (environmental, social, governance) industry has created a market that is rapidly growing, channeling many trillions of dollars into so-called sustainable or responsible investments.

As Pericles, one of the most influential statesmen in the history of Greece, pointed out some 2,500 years ago: *It is not our task to predict the future, but to be well prepared for it.* As Bruce Piasecki notes, we must, in a sense, make these corporate giants our own, for they manufacture our future.

Michael Spanos
Founder and Managing Partner, Global Sustain

Preface

During my thirty years as a management consultant to over a hundred firms, my team and I have been able to implement a number of changes that have helped international companies like Toyota, Suncor, Siemens, and FedEx transform themselves into *new world companies*—companies that are ready to take on the challenges of today's global economy. In doing this, I have formulated a way to describe how corporations mature by seeing the process as a symbolic hour-long clock of corporate competitiveness. As this concept evolved, I came to focus not on the clock itself, but on what it represents: time. Further, I broke down the time periods into increments that represent important stages in the life of a corporation. I often refer to these stages as "urgencies," because, as I see it, corporations must accomplish the business goals outlined within each time period if they are to be successful.

Over time, I have revised my description of these stages in a company's life to take into account the emergence of what I call *social response capitalism*, the subject of this book. I became increasingly aware of the financial implications of social response capitalism while working with the new world companies that are spotlighted in this book. You will come to see how each one contributes to the most important new business movement in decades, and why this movement is crucial to the health of any company—whether a large global corporation or a small regional family business.

THE SIX STAGES OF A CORPORATION'S LIFE

The first of the six stages in the life of a corporation can be summed up by the term "profit margin improvement." In this initial stage, increasing revenues and profits is of primary importance for success.

During the second stage of a corporation's life, company practices must focus on improving efficiency in the areas of manufacturing, distribution, and sales. The keys for efficient manufacturing include improving and increasing the automation of the manufacturing process, as well as finding outsourcers who can reduce production costs. A company's sales and distribution functions can generate as much as 80 percent of its profits, and what has become known as *distribution channel realignment* is a key area in which corporations can significantly improve performance. This may include such strategies as broadening networks, reducing warehouse and transportation costs, and improving customer service.

Improved performance leads to the third stage of a corporation's life: expansion of its global customer base. Successful corporations must grow globally if they hope to remain competitive. Growth may not be the "mother of invention," but it certainly is the "sister."

Assuming a corporation manages a successful third phase—and only a few do—its fourth stage must focus on *product differentiation*. In the extremely competitive environment of international business, corporations must continually improve the recognizability of their products against those of their competitors. Once that goal has been reached, the corporation enters the fifth stage, which involves reducing various risk factors for investors. Whatever corporations produce, they must do so with fewer operational and financial risks than their competitors.

Finally, the sixth and final stage of a successful corporation focuses on environmental, social, and governance practices—three areas of concern that lie outside company operations. Simply put, this recently evolved stage involves a company's efforts in responding to the *social concerns* of its customer and clients, and having these actions recognized by the analysts and investment managers who assess its likelihood of success.

This is the concept of social response capitalism. I'll have much more to say about this in the Introduction and the chapters that follow. For now, let me say that one of the most important ways to evaluate a company's prospects and performance rests with its *social product differentiation*, which involves the integration of "social response values" into its products and services. Over time, as I've refined my approach to corporate success by adding social concerns as measurable criteria, I've come to realize that this sixth stage is necessary not only for corporate success, but also for corporate survival.

Unless a firm takes into account the profound changes that have become part of the new global corporate culture, it can neither thrive nor can it survive.

In *New World Companies*, it is my goal to provide you with new tools to gauge corporate success in the coming years. Within the chapters that follow, I will spotlight a number of companies that embody these principles in bold defiance of the highly speculative short-term form of capitalism that has dominated American business for so long.

New World Companies

Introduction

Redefining Capitalism in a World of Seven Billion Souls

here are several questions that have been on my mind for years: Is it possible to identify and isolate a new set of core principles that demonstrate how companies must incorporate socially responsive practices into their operations as they compete in an increasingly uncertain global business environment? And once done, is it possible to tie these principles directly to quantifiable measures of stock and societal value?

When I use the term "quantifiable measures," I am referring to such areas as increased revenues and profits, improved efficiency, and an expanded global customer base. These measures, however, are not limited to financial performance.

Let me expand on this idea.

The way in which a corporation responds in three areas—environmental concerns, social issues that affect people throughout the world, and the quality and integrity of its governance team—is becoming more and more important. The success of a business, once defined exclusively by profitability, is now moving toward a process that also takes into account its concern for the needs of people everywhere.

This has come about with the development of environmental, social, and governance (ESG) metrics. These measures or criteria have become the basis of an expanded way of understanding and evaluating the principles, practices, and performance of corporations. They are the three areas around which *social response capitalism* coalesces, and they now stand alongside profit as key criteria for corporate success. Here is a brief and basic overview of these areas:

■ Environmental

Environmental criteria take into account a company's energy use, waste, pollution, natural resource conservation, and animal treatment. They also evaluate which environmental risks might affect a company's income and how the company is managing those challenges. For example, a company would be evaluated on how it manages such environmental challenges as the ownership of contaminated land, its responsibility for an oil spill, its disposal of hazardous waste, its management of toxic emissions, or its compliance with the government's environmental regulations.

■ Social

Social criteria involve the company's business relationships. Does it work with suppliers who hold the same values that the company itself claims to hold? Does the company donate a percentage of its profits to the community or perform volunteer work? Do the company's working conditions show a high regard for its employees' health and safety? Are the interests of shareholders taken into consideration?

■ Governance

With regard to governance, investors want to know that a company uses accurate and transparent accounting methods, and that common stockholders are allowed to vote on important issues. They also want companies to avoid conflicts of interest in their choice of board members. Finally, they prefer not to invest in companies that engage in illegal behavior or use political contributions to obtain favorable treatment. In addition, governance criteria also takes into account how thoroughly the company's management makes decisions on the welfare of its employees and the degree to which it is involved in the development of key corporate policies.

Corporations need to direct their focus on ESG metrics in order to achieve and improve their financial performance, as well as to create a culture that responds to the most pressing needs of the people they serve. I use the word "serve" advisedly; in a real sense, corporations are evolving into public servants who address not only the needs of their shareholders, but also the needs of the seven billion people of this world.

THE IMPACT OF ESG ON GLOBAL BUSINESS

Despite the great variance in cultures, languages, and politics around the world, ESG metrics are becoming a growing part of the universal measure of corporate success. Thanks to their inclusion into business practices, we are finding that the voices of all the people on this planet are being heard. And the new world companies described in this book are among the growing number of firms that are listening. By taking these metrics into account, corporations—in addition to enhancing their financial well-being—are gaining significant value in terms of their ability to respond socially to the needs of the world's citizens.

What's really fascinating is that throughout the world (and my business has taken me to countries on four continents), the principles I've outlined in this book are being adopted by a growing number of global corporations. Environmental-, social-, and governance-based measures are increasingly being taken into account as customers, investors, and analysts define what matters in the way corporations conduct their business.

While profit is obviously necessary for corporate survival, the attention to profitability must now share its place in the corporate hierarchy with what is coming to be recognized as *sustainable value*—the incorporation of ESG metrics into a company's philosophy. The growing inclusion of ESG values into analysts' assessments makes it clear that corporate success is starting to be seen as a much longer-term social process. The transition from focusing on quarterly and annual reports to viewing corporate success in the long term is one of the key focuses of this book.

In effect, as the business community is being transformed from a multi-national culture in which hundreds of languages are spoken to a global culture, we are increasingly requiring that corporations adopt as one of their mottoes: "ESG Practiced and Spoken Here."

As it stands now, the ESG principles and practices associated with social response capitalism are, in fact, becoming part of the analyses of corporate performance by scholars, investment managers, business analysts, and social commentators. (Unfortunately, when it comes to social responsibility, the media tends to focus on what businesses are doing wrong, rather than on the benefits they gain when behaving with intelligent responsiveness.) Incorporating the fundamentals of social response capitalism enables firms to grow and thrive in today's global business environment.

THE PEOPLE PRINCIPLE

In his book *Small Is Beautiful* British economist E. F. Schumacher advises businesses to practice "economics as if people mattered."

By these words, Schumacher led me to understand that business is not solely about price and quality or the management science of optimization; ultimately, it is about people. This principle has been important in my understanding of social response capitalism, and I've come to believe that making this principle central to the way companies conduct business will enable them to improve their potential for success, as well as the quality of life of the people who work for, invest in, and patronize them.

Corporations of all types represent what I see as the most powerful and influential shapers of behavior at every level that exists on this planet . . . for better or for worse.

From the freedom and initiatives they give their employees, to the quality of their products, to the good they do for their clients and customers, businesses must take the lead in managing resources and responding to the world's mounting social needs as they compete for investment capital. Corporations must seek to provide solutions in all significant areas—including food and energy supplies, information technology, health care, and transportation—for the more than seven billion citizens of this world.

As we look toward a future in which we understand our shared responsibility for improving the lives of our brothers and sisters around the world, it is my strong conviction that social response capitalism has become the most important force for good on this planet. By exploring the in-depth meaning of this term in the chapters that follow, I hope to change the focus of anyone who has an interest in how corporations define their responsibilities. This group includes corporate officers who define the culture, policies, and practices of the companies they run, to the analysts and brokers who examine these businesses in an effort to assess their value and predict their stock worth and success. It also includes the consumers, who purchase the goods and services these companies provide. Even beyond that, though, because international businesses today have such a profound and far-reaching influence on how we manage our resources, every person in the world is affected, directly or indirectly, by the level of social responsibility practiced by these global giants.

In redefining the way businesses can and should practice social response capitalism, I am broadening the term "social responsibility" significantly. As you read on, you will better understand what this term means and how it can evolve to create a much bigger umbrella than has been articulated to this point. By integrating the principles and practices associated with this concept into corporate business policies, you will see how new world companies can dramatically improve their performance in measurable ways—ways that incorporate sustainable, value-based practices into their business models.

MISPLACED PRIORITIES

Let me share a statistic that demonstrates how important it is for businesses to focus on ESG metrics if they are to succeed in the growing global business community. Since 1981, more than 60 percent of Fortune 500 companies have either gone out of business or have been significantly downgraded in size, influence, and/or governance structures. Many have had to sell off parts of their businesses, which, in some cases, were the very brands on which they had built their success.

The fact that the majority of these once vibrant Fortune 500 companies have lost so much ground clearly demonstrates that the critical elements of social response capitalism impact the people who work for and patronize these companies. The overwhelming reason that these corporations failed is because they did not adapt to the global corporate culture that was becoming more aligned with ESG principles and practices.

I have come to view this planet as a new world in which corporations are in a position to transform what many see as an increasingly limited world into one of unlimited possibilities—a transformation that can occur through the adoption of social response business policies and practices.

New world companies that follow these practices are much more likely to prosper and grow than firms that ignore them. My company's team has been able to bring about positive change in the corporate behavior of a large number of companies—many of which are reviewed in this book. The reason I am telling you this is because today I feel more strongly about my convictions regarding sustainability and social responsiveness than when I started my company in 1981.

THE PURPOSE OF THIS BOOK

My primary purpose in writing this book is to lay out a practical blueprint for companies throughout the world to adopt socially responsive corporate practices as an integral part of their operations. This is not simply because shareholders will benefit as bottom lines are improved, but also because the lives of those who buy and use the products and services will be positively affected. And, as you will see, in an indirect way, the lives of our fellow citizens will experience valuable results as well.

My blueprint is also designed to show investors how to analyze a company's philosophies and corporate practices. This will help make them aware if the business supports sound practices that will improve its chance of success. They will gain a better understanding of the connection between adopting the principles of social response capitalism and increasing a firm's sustained value, its connection to and alignment with key social stakeholders, and its future prospects.

It is important for consumers to assert their influence on companies, insisting that they follow the best practices in this new world. No longer should it be acceptable for corporations *not* to follow the business practices presented in this book. The approval and support of customers and clients, reflected in how they choose from the extraordinary variety of available products and services, is one of the most influential ways of making sure their interests are being served.

What's Ahead

Throughout this book I have focused on a number of key new world companies that exemplify the best of this new breed of corporations. Among those discussed include energy innovators FedEx and Suncor, and Caterpillar, which, in addition to being a socially responsible product development company, is also a pioneer in the social and governance areas. Flex (formerly Flextronics)—what I call a behind-the-scenes new world company—is involved in the manufacture of products in so many different areas that I have referred to it in numerous places throughout the book.

I consider the heart of *New World Companies* as my *operational handbook for understanding the new world of global business.* Those in the military might call this "shared actionable intelligence." I call it "How Firms Must Compete."

Chapter 1, "The World on Your Wrist," explains the role that digital technology has had in generating what can be called a true information explosion. It is this phenomenon that allows consumers to access unlimited amounts of data on just about any subject, including that of corporations. And that information enables anyone to demand that companies become ESG-conscious entities. This chapter further explains how this movement toward cultural and global realignment is instrumental in bringing the people of the world together toward a new era of human rights.

Chapter 2 provides an extensive discussion on what I see as the key component of the ESG trio: the environment. The reason I find this to be the centerpiece of any discussion on ESG metrics is because the environment is inseparably linked to energy. A successful transition to an ESG-aware economy cannot occur without the awareness of how we can make the transition from carbon-based fuels, including oil, natural gas, and coal, to alternative sources of energy.

While alternatives are certainly a key to improving our environment, we are currently in a period of transition from the dense energy of fossil fuels to the more diffuse sources of energy generated by wind and solar power. The global economy cannot continue to operate unless we are able to gradually develop the technologies that allow us to generate energy in amounts equivalent to—and eventually much greater than—what we are able to produce today through carbon-based fuels. So this chapter points out how we can make our conventional energy production much more environmentally sound while focusing attention on the responsible development of replacement energy sources.

Chapter 3 continues the discussion of ESG metrics by examining what I call the "people principles"—the *social* and *governance* criteria of the emerging ESG awareness. I briefly catalog some of the high points in the evolution of these areas, then further explore what each represents. I also introduce one of the key reporting agencies that brings to light corporate behavior in these two important areas, and then explore how "corporate mansions" have been irrevocably changed by an increased focus on social and governance metrics—a change that includes the emergence of the chief relationship officer (CRO). Concluding this chapter is an eye-opening look at how we are evolving from a "buyer beware" environment into one that is "buyer be heard."

I like to refer to Chapters 4 and 5 as the "money chapters." No matter how successfully we integrate ESG metrics into our analytics and into the policies and practices of corporations, in the words of songwriter Randy Newman, "It's money that matters."

Chapter 4 presents a financial profile of the past forty years, explaining how speculative capitalism gained power as the focus of business became ever more concentrated on money alone. At the same time, though, what has now become social response capitalism gradually began to get its message out to the investment community. You will see how its principles have already begun reversing the economic decline brought about by speculative capitalism. An extensive discussion of ESG metrics demonstrates how these criteria have evolved from difficult-to-measure "intangibles" into concrete components that are increasingly being factored into corporate policies and investor decisions.

The focus in Chapter 5 is how ESG metrics has led to the most successful long-term investment practices. You will discover the prime movers in the ESG investment community, and learn how these criteria are now becoming available to investors and analysts as they determine the worth and likely success of the companies they monitor.

"The social response future is now" is the message of Chapter 6, which takes a behind-the-scenes look at Toyota—one of the world's most successful corporations and the largest automobile manufacturer. You will see how Toyota led the way in social response product development and became the standard-bearer for ESG principles. Its corporate culture has become one of the models for responsive social and governance corporate practices.

What I Hope to Accomplish

By taking a new look at how global companies operate in today's interconnected world, we can help chart the course of a sustainable future for the planet on which we live. In the end, I hope to define the term "new world companies" in such a way that you will understand how to approach, invest in, and choose products from them. I want you to understand how these companies are positioned to create a new future—one in which the people of the world can participate directly in improving corporate behavior and its impact on society. In the process, this book reinforces how today's electronically interconnected world now allows us to participate in making better products in a better world. Social response capitalism is based on "the many," not the lucky few or the isolated financial elites. With that said, let's see what the future has already brought us.

1

The World on Your Wrist

On Our Way to
a Global Community

With its 2015 debut, the Apple Watch gave us a new and innovative way to keep in touch with the world. Cartoon detective Dick Tracy may have introduced an early version of this watch with his two-way wrist radio in 1945, but it took Apple, along with the digital revolution that has occurred since the mid-1990s, to make it a reality. Beyond giving people everywhere the ability to simply communicate with others, Apple has provided them with the opportunity to wear *"their world on their wrist."*

Digital technology in general allows us to personalize our worlds in ways that hadn't been possible just two decades ago. Beyond personalization, though, this latest innovative product means that we won't even have to reach into our pockets or purses to pull out a smart phone when we want to check the time, read emails, or follow the stocks we've invested in. And beyond that, we need look no further than our wrists to send messages to the principals of companies on which the success of our 401(k) depends. These innovations have brought in the "new world."

In the coming years, the Apple Watch and other such devices are likely to gain widespread favor because of the relentless push toward globalization that has followed in the wake of the rapid evolution of digital technology. This trend has led toward the realization that environmental, social, and governance (ESG) metrics or measurements are among the major keys to global corporate success. As this becomes even clearer in the coming years, wearing such a device may become not just a participatory right, but a necessity as well.

One of the subjects explored in this chapter involves the distinction between corporate multi-nationalism and globalism. *Corporate multi-nationalism* prioritizes profits over human and material resources. *Globalism*, on the other hand, is characterized by a company's adoption of ESG values that remain consistent in all of the countries in which they do business. Truly global corporations are spreading the message of environmental, social, and governance responsibility around the globe, regardless of the countries with which they are dealing.

This chapter discusses the impact of digital technology in bringing us out of a world that has been comprised of hundreds of nation-states into a world that has become a global consumer community. This is being achieved through the ongoing spread of positive values through business practices that have evolved and been broadly adopted during the past several decades. This process is, in fact, the foundation on which this book is built. At the heart of this dramatic shift is the "information explosion" that is occurring throughout the world; this abundance of accessible data is the phenomenon that is spurring our transformation from a multi-national culture into a global one.

The increasing adoption of ESG values by the global corporate culture is a move that is capable of bringing the citizens and countries of the world together, rather than pitting them against each other. This ongoing shift from multi-national corporations to truly global companies can lead to the restoration of peaceful and productive competition throughout the world.

THE INFORMATION EXPLOSION

As a young family member once told me, "My generation doesn't care about the politics of nothing. We want things that work well and work fast. We see a universe of exchange before us, not the walls and wars of past nation-states." During the 1990s, the Internet—and the instantaneous global communications that came along for the ride—put swiftness into globalization, moving us rapidly toward the world of "things that work well and work fast." This began the significant social process of confirming that the profit-is-the-only-thing-that-matters worldview was too out-of-date to survive much longer.

Enhanced globalization is a direct result of our ability to exchange information with everyone from fellow employees and shareholders to analysts and investors to customers and clients. It means that consumers are becoming increasingly more knowledgeable, sophisticated, and particular about the products they buy—from cars and computers to the homes they live in. Although cost is always an important factor, it may no longer be the single most important reason for purchasing the products of one company over another's. Today, information on the companies themselves—the quality of their products and services, their social contributions, ethics, and environmental concerns—disseminated through blogs and online reviews, now have great impact on a person's buying decisions. This profound global phenomenon is a key factor in the emergence of new world companies.

This dramatic increase in the scope and power of digital information technology over the past two decades has been unprecedented in human history. Consider the following fact: More than five billion of the seven billion people now living on our planet use digital mobile phones to call, text, tweet, and browse the Internet—even if that means sharing one device among family members and friends. In other words, five out of every seven people in the world are capable of electronically communicating person-to-person with each other.

To further illustrate this point, a few years ago, I was sightseeing in Bath, England. As I approached one of the city's ancient Roman bathhouses, my daughter was simultaneously watching YouTube videos on her phone at home. She connected me (and several of her friends) to the video of a boy in Bath, who was comically speaking in his best imitation of New York, Texas, and British accents.

When it comes to accurately describing the amount of data that is created, captured, and stored using digital technology, we have had to create new words. Take the word "gigabyte," for instance. While the term once represented an astonishing amount of data, it is now almost obsolete. Many of the new terms are themselves rapidly becoming insignificant in the face of an unprecedented information overload. "Terabytes," for instance, which refers to a trillion bytes or a thousand gigabytes, has became virtually meaningless due to the data onslaught we have experienced in the past few years alone. We have had to coin new words like "petabyte," "exabyte," and "zettabyte" to describe new volumes of information being created each day via the digital technology explosion. Each of these terms represents a volume of information that is significantly larger than its predecessor.

As Professor Winston Hide at the Harvard School of Public Health recently explained, "In the last five years, more scientific data has been generated than in the entire history of mankind." According to a statement made in 2010 by Google CEO Eric Schmidt, "Every two days we create as much information as we did from the dawn of civilization up to the year 2003." Let's just say that the rate of data creation hasn't slowed down since then. In 2012, an estimated 2.5 exabytes of data were being created every day, and that number has been doubling every month since then.

It's not just the massive amounts of digital data that are being created, captured, and shared that is important. It's that last word, "shared," that holds the key, the final piece of the puzzle in the creation of a truly global economy. There is an old saying, "All politics is local." When we substitute the word "businesses" for the word "politics," we get a sense of what a profound change has been emerging in the scope and responsiveness of global corporations in the digital age.

Indeed, in an important sense, all business is now local—and the planet is the new local.

Digital technology now enables us to share information instantly through those extraordinary communication devices that we now carry in our pockets and wear on our wrists. We can transfer cash around the world instantaneously or share images generated by unmanned probes hundreds of millions of miles away in the vast reaches of space. A significant and growing percentage of people around the world now have access to information that was once available only to those wielding political and/or economic power.

In the wake of this technological explosion, at roughly the same time Apple released its revolutionary watch, it reported the largest net income of any public company in the history of mankind. To date, this computer and communications pioneer has sold more than a billion iPhones, iPads, and iPods since it launched the product lines less than a decade ago.

CROSSING THE GREAT CULTURAL DIVIDES

To better understand where we hope to go, it is helpful to take a look at where we have been. For over five thousand years, our planet has given rise to thousands of diverse cultures. Beginning as clans, then villages, and eventually distinct societies, these groups developed their own languages, religious beliefs, customs, cuisines, social habits, and the list goes on. Some cultures were relatively isolated, while others developed within closer proximity to one another. As we can see from history, both ancient and modern, these cultural differences often gave rise to conflict—from one city-state battling with another to societies that were intent on dominating the world. While history is certainly replete with warfare, it has also shown that when nations join together, they can create stable environments in which they are able to prosper and grow—at least for a time.

By the end of War World II, the United States and its Allies had thousands of troops stationed throughout the world. After seven long years as a battleground, the world, in a sense, had become a much smaller place. Over the next fifty years, as communication systems improved, as the ability to travel to remote destinations expanded, and as the knowledge of other cultures increased, governments throughout the world began to recognize the importance of international trade for improving their economies and strengthening their nations. To a great extent, they encouraged the development of companies that reflected their own national needs and values.

Just as the cultural differences between nations had played out on the battlefields, the conflict between corporations vying for resources, manufacturing facilities, and sales resulted in both a lack of ethical behavior, and indifference toward the welfare of the very people they worked with and for. As these companies grew, extending their operations from one country to another, they became large multi-national corporations—corporations whose primary focus was on making profits no matter what the social ramifications.

Today, however, the digital world has transformed a number of forward-thinking companies into what can be described as new world companies. This transformation, as you will see, has occurred for many reasons. For one, nations as well as businesses live in glass houses. They may succeed in hiding behind drawn curtains for a while; however it is the people working with these entities who now have immediate communication with countless others around the world. It is these new world companies that are embracing the ESG values.

BENEFITS OF THE NEW GLOBALISM

In an important sense, globalization and digital technology are inseparable. The Apple Watch, for instance, is the latest landmark product in a long line of digital information-sharing tools that continues to boost the speed, power, and convenience of our access to the world—a world that had remained relatively inaccessible to us until the early 1990s.

Such extraordinary technological advances are effectively bringing people around the world together in stunning new ways, while exponentially increasing their interdependency. As a result of the information revolution, what have been known as *multinational* corporations are now transforming themselves into *global* corporations. And with that transformation, we are witnessing the gradual change from a multi-national world into one that is globally interdependent. It is not only products and services that are "going global," but cultures and economics as well.

One of the most obvious benefits of this transformation can be summed up in the word "interconnectedness." Thanks to digital technology, we can communicate almost instantly with anyone in virtually any location. I use the word "virtually" advisedly. In one sense, we can wear a "virtual world" on our wrists; in another— and more important sense—the virtual world of products and services is now almost seamlessly connected to the real world. We can access information about products, order and pay for them instantly, and have them delivered to our door . . . all without leaving the comfort of our homes.

While we are becoming interconnected, thanks to the technologically mediated exchange of goods, we are also experiencing an exchange of cultures and cultural values. Through the digital miracles at our fingertips (or on our wrists), the more we are exposed to other people and their cultures, the more we are becoming global citizens—part of an increasingly unified global culture based on shared values. This merger of the virtual world with the real one is an extraordinary benefit of this trend.

This "new world globalism" enables and encourages so-called developing nations to speed up the process of improving the lives of their citizens. I see this as the gradual diminishing of the age of multi-national corporations. It is an age characterized by the exploitation of developing nations by international companies that have established facilities in these countries and have taken advantage of the low labor costs. Now, it is clear that as the movement from multi-nationalism into a fuller phase of globalism improves, so does the quality of life for the citizens of these easily exploited countries. Through their connection with global countries, developing nations are now experiencing increased interactions with the greater world, and this is resulting in numerous positive changes. According to the International Monetary Fund (IMF):

> There is substantial evidence, from countries of different sizes and different regions, that as countries "globalize" their citizens benefit, in the form of access to a wider variety of goods and services, lower prices, more and better-paying jobs, improved health, and higher overall living standards. It is probably no mere coincidence that over the past twenty years, as a number of countries have become more open to global economic forces, the percentage of the developing world living in extreme poverty—defined as living on less than $1 per day—has been cut in half.

And while many critics of globalization base their arguments on the notion that globalism "weakens national sovereignty," I argue that becoming part of what media guru Marshall McLuhan described as "the global village" is actually the key to eliminating the borders that have so often been the excuse for war and mistrust and replacing them with shared cultural and economic advances.

Another notable benefit of the growing global nature of corporate cultures involves construction. When corporations invest in the building of facilities in developing countries, they are encouraging the spread of the very technology that is at the root of the new globalism. This process brings with it increased financial stability along with a workforce that is experienced and educated, and, therefore, better equipped to participate in the global economy. The more a country is able to participate in the global economy, the faster it is able to escape its third-world status.

There is still a great deal to be accomplished. About a third of the seven billion citizens of the world earn less than $2 a day. While informed critics use this statistic to argue that globalism is not achieving sufficient desired results, as I see it, participating in the global economy is still an effective path in leading underdeveloped countries away from poverty.

No longer are sophisticated communication tools, the ready availability of global transportation, and the exchange of goods and services across borders and oceans limited to wealthy individuals or nations. Many people who had once been consigned to living isolated, impoverished lives, are now being given the tools for discovering the greater world out there and all it has to offer—a world that they are closer to enjoying. It is something they would not have even considered just a few decades ago.

The expansion of information through technology has enabled the emergence of what I call "markets without borders" on an enormous scale. This new business environment has become an arena in which new world companies can benefit financially, while at the same time becoming benefactors to people everywhere. Chapter 3 presents a detailed discussion on the various people affected by the "social" metric that drives so many socially responsive companies.

Corporations can benefit enormously from the new globalism because it enables them to standardize their products and services as different cultures and the demands of various nations become more and more similar. The same goes for how they produce, market, and distribute their products, all of which result in significant price reductions for so many now-globalized goods and services.

One thing is certain: We are nearing the end of multi-national businesses with the replacement of truly global "new world companies."

THE PATH TO GLOBALISM

The path to globalism is not without its impediments. Although the ongoing march to a global corporate community has been moving forward, the economic crash of 2008 (discussed at length in Chapters 4 and 5) has been the major source of a slowdown in that progress. One commentator sees this slowdown of economic globalism as giving rise to the emergence of "guarded globalization." Believing that they are targets of corporations that are looking after only their own interests, some developing countries are becoming wary of opening more industries to multi-national companies. They are becoming increasingly reluctant to give up control to large companies over increasing segments of their improving economies. This is seen as the "politicization" of economic policy, with a significant change of focus to the targeted countries' national interests and their economic sovereignty.

The process of globalization is being thwarted because "financial services, information technology, telecommunications, and food sectors have all been politicized. . . . The state perceives more and more sectors to be of strategic importance and deters foreign companies from entering them. Indeed, the rise of state capitalism in some of the world's most important emerging markets has shifted the tectonic plates. . . . Globalization now comes with new costs and risks."

Establishing truly free markets in countries whose governments tend to be autocratic is becoming more difficult. If markets are the key force in deciding how economic policies are determined, centralized governmental power is threatened. This does not sit well with those in power, and it can impede the likelihood of such countries freely joining in the new globalist economy. It means that they will not realize the many benefits such a move could mean for their citizens. Here is how foreign policy analyst Ian Bremmer explains it:

> Whereas the free market system's motive of maximizing profits and growth is economic, state capitalism's goal is political: to control economic development and thereby maximize the incumbent regime's chances of survival. It isn't a coherent philosophy but a set of techniques peculiar to each country.

We are learning that globalization is not a one-size-fits-all process, and that despite the merging of many cultural and political ideologies that characterize the new globalism, the process of interconnectedness is still under construction. There are many bridges that remain to be built.

THE SHARING ECONOMY
NEW ENGINES OF SOCIAL CAPITAL

Among the most intriguing aspects of the new globalism is what has been termed "the sharing economy." The computerization of our lives has caused the decentralization of many business activities that were once considered standard. This has led to the inspiration of new and ingenious ways to create businesses. At times, this is done with very little capital investment because the capital assets are already in existence. Budding entrepreneurs are now finding ways to exploit these assets, often for completely different purposes than originally intended. The Internet and social media are integral keys to their success. Airbnb, a company that has turned houses, apartments, and other spaces into income-generating opportunities for property owners, is one example of this new type of business. Uber, a car service that has redefined the word "taxi," is another.

AIRBNB

At one time, houses and apartments were seen almost exclusively as places where people lived. Now, thanks to Airbnb (shortened from AirBed & Breakfast), they are being transformed into rentable lodgings for travelers to use during their vacations and business trips.

Airbnb's unassuming start occurred in October of 2007. At the time, two San Francisco residents, Brian Chesky and Joe Gebbia, were having difficulty paying the rent on the apartment they shared. When they discovered that a convention in the city had caused a hotel room shortage, they decided to put three inflated air mattresses in their living room and rent them out. After advertising themselves on the Internet as an "AirBed and Breakfast," the two had no problem renting the space (which included a home-made breakfast) and paying their rent.

The successful undertaking blossomed into a multi-billion dollar business that became the Internet listing agent for people all over the world to either rent or rent out accommodations—from airbeds and shared spaces to entire homes and apartments, boats, castles, igloos, private islands, and other properties.

The company grew at an extraordinary pace to the point where it has service providers in more than 34,000 cities in 190 countries worldwide. Over 25 million guests have logged onto Airbnb.com to find lodgings during their travels. By the end of 2014, Airbnb had become the largest "hotel" company in the world by one measure, with more than a million rooms available to rent. Its nearest competitors, InterContinental, Hilton, and Marriott, each had fewer than 700,000 rooms to rent. Airbnb currently provides more than 17 percent of all hotel rooms in New York City, nearly 12 percent in Paris, and more than 10 percent in London.

UBER

When most people think of taxicabs, they picture yellow transportation vehicles that are flagged down on city streets. Today, a company called Uber offers a new type of car service. Through its mobile app, Uber allows people to hail drivers and pay for rides with their smartphones. Passengers can even share their ride with others who are traveling to the same area. Further, Uber gives approved drivers the opportunity to generate income by using their own vehicles to transport passengers.

This new approach for connecting riders with drivers began in San Francisco in 2009, around the same time that Airbnb was starting. A pair of entrepreneurs, Travis Kalanick and Garrett Camp, started UberCab. Kalanick, who had attended a convention in Paris a short time earlier, came up with the idea while trying to flag down a cab there. What started in 2009 as an online limousine service, gradually morphed into a much broader car service called Uber in 2010. The company's smartphone app not only offers riders a quick and convenient way to hail cabs (without having to stand in the rain), it also enables drivers to avoid the licensing and registrations associated with the taxi industry. In less than five years, Uber had expanded to more than a hundred cities in forty-five countries and was valued at nearly $20 billion.

Although businesses like Uber and Airbnb have been the target of regulators and have faced lawsuits and negative reviews, their success is undeniable. Such smartphone app- and software-based companies reflect the incredible entrepreneurship of aspiring businesspeople who understand the unlimited possibilities of having "the world on your wrist." They allow us to help our family, friends, and firms in more efficient ways.

"COLLABORATIVE CONSUMPTION"

The emergence of Uber, Airbnb, and many other similar if lesser known Internet-enabled companies has led business analyst Rachel Botsman to coin the phrase "collaborative consumption." As Botsman sees it, collaborative consumption—known by some as "the sharing economy"—is a way to make money through "underused assets," such as homes in the case of Airbnb and cars in the case of Uber.

Finding new ways to generate money through existing underused assets is now expanding into industries like healthcare, insurance, and financial services. It is estimated that for these industries, as much as $14 billion is lost annually due to inefficient use of available assets.

One example of this sort of collaboration is done through Cohealo, a software application that encourages sharing within healthcare systems. For instance, through the practice of sharing expensive medical equipment among organizations, healthcare providers are able to use the equipment without having to purchase it. Such applications of intelligent sharing increase efficiency while reducing capital and maintenance costs. This type of sharing is becoming one of the key principles of social response capitalism.

This business space is expanding to include companies that enable not only the sharing of equipment, but also the sharing of services. It is already becoming established in the areas of identity verification and e-commerce payments. For processing payments over the Internet, the company Stripe now provides online payment services of "billions of dollars a year for thousands of businesses in eighteen countries around the world," according to the company's CEO Patrick Collison.

BITCOINS

While precious metals such as gold and silver have been a universal means of exchange between countries for centuries, the digital age has given rise to a new form of international currency called *crypto-currency*. It is an alternative—specifically digital—type of currency.

The bitcoin, launched in 2009, is the first decentralized digital currency. It is Internet-based money whose value is determined by the market of buyers and sellers, and which can be used to make payments through transferring virtual currency over the Internet. The key to bitcoin's importance is that transactions using it are direct and not traceable by regulatory agencies, and they are not subject to the fees that banks and credit card companies charge users.

By late 2015, the total market capitalization for the roughly 100 crypto-currencies then in circulation was just under $4 billion. Nearly 90 percent of the total market capitalization was held by bitcoin.

There are a number of reasons that interest in alternative currencies is growing. In addition to allowing users to avoid the added costs of making transactions through banks and credit cards, crypto-currencies allow online transactions without revealing any personal data, such as account or credit card information. In addition, they allow many people in the developing world without access to banks to make financial transactions through cell phones.

Currently, the use of bitcoins is new and open to abuse and misuse. Bitcoins do, however, indicate the mounting likelihood of a more universal and instant currency in the near future. This enhanced means of exchange, with fewer tariffs, taxes, and banking intermediaries, should enable more new world companies over time.

THE NEW DIRECTION OF INTERCONNECTED "THINGS"

With the emergence of radically new twenty-first century businesses, we are witnessing "an early clue to the new direction." As Rachel Botsman explains it, within a matter of only a few years, collaborative consumption in the sharing economy "will just become the way of thinking about creating value, deploying assets, and interacting with people. There will be many other billion-dollar companies in this space that will help people realize that this idea will disrupt the way a lot of industries operate."

Beyond that, though, analyst Larry Getlen explains how pervasive the world on our wrist will become:

> According to author Samuel Greengard, "'The Internet of Things' represents a more evolved and advanced state where physical and digital worlds are blended into a single space." We will soon exist, he says, in a single, technologically connected ecosystem with all the physical items in our lives, from refrigerators and microwave ovens to our cars, wired into each other. He quotes networking firm Cisco Systems as stating that "more than 1.5 trillion 'things' exist in the physical world, and 99 percent of physical objects will eventually become part of a network."

CONCLUSION

It is clear to me that without the digital revolution, the ESG revolution that we are experiencing now would not exist. Without the availability of the world in digital form, we would not be experiencing the positive benefits made by global corporations to the environment or to issues of social and governance policies and practices.

Among the most important matters that have resulted from this revolution is the focus on human rights. And one of the most important rights we have is the right to an Internet Protocol (IP) address. This address is a singular numerical combination that is assigned to every digital device—computers, printers, smartphones, tablets, etc.—that is part of a computer network. When you have an IP address, you also have the ability to communicate electronically with anyone anywhere on the planet. In that important sense, digital technology represents nothing less than freedom.

When I use the word "freedom," I'm not just referring to freedom of information. Because of the dramatic increases in the speed of and the advancements in digital communications technology, we can travel electronically to many places and help contribute to solving many problems. Thanks to the omnipresence of computers—the extraordinary volume of information they can process and the lightning speed at which it can be distributed—we are able to participate in and influence the practices and policies of corporations around the world in ways that were unheard of only a few decades ago.

This emerging new world is not without significant problems. Crypto-currencies such as the bitcoin, for instance, can provide access to a system of exchange that allows people to purchase products around the world. However, because it is unregulated, it can be used to make purchases of everything from illegal drugs to covert weapons. While I believe it is important that we are all free to make purchases without being monitored by an overreaching government, at the same time, those purchases can sometimes be as dangerous to our freedoms as a dictatorial government. For example, in an ironic twist, many forces committed to the destruction of Western civilization are using the very technology created by the same civilizations they are committed to eliminating.

As you will see in the upcoming chapters, digital technology has spawned a new era of companies whose employees sit in front of computers and are involved with equity trading that create profits out of thin air, profits that have nothing to do with what is important in our real-world lives. That said, there is no doubt in my mind that the role being played by digital technology in spreading the values and practices that inform new world companies is overwhelmingly positive. These better products enable a better world.

New world companies are now positioned to create enormous beneficial changes in all of our lives—including those of the world's poorest citizens, whose governments have too often proven unable or unwilling to do so. Companies that implement and manage the creation and exchange of goods and services creatively, responsibly, and efficiently are leading this charge. They are real-world companies that make our lives better through the practice of social response capitalism—the key not only to corporate success in the coming decades, but also to the future of capitalism.

2

The Matter of Energy

Innovation, Information, and Sustainable Value

The key role that environmental, social, and governance (ESG) standards play in the development of social response capitalism was presented in the Introduction. Chapter 1 showed how the new globalized economy has set the stage for this type of capitalism to flourish. The focus of this chapter is on what is considered the most important and difficult component of the environmental metric in the ESG trinity: energy. Why energy? Because it is energy, not money, that makes the world go round. And it is our consumption of energy that threatens the very future of our planet.

Carbon—the building block of life—is the fifteenth most common element on earth and the second most common element in the human body. Although carbon is a key component of all living things, it also has the potential to cause unprecedented destruction. According to the World Bank, unless severe restrictions are placed on the release of carbon dioxide (CO_2) and CO_2 equivalents, a potentially dangerous temperature increase of 4°C over pre-industrial levels is likely. Even this seemingly small change in global temperature could prove disastrous. If this increase occurs, and many predict it will, scientists who are monitoring global warming tell us that we will be struggling to adapt to coastal flooding, agricultural shifts, and severe weather.

Yet there is hope not only from the inventiveness of socially responsive firms, but also from the commitment of activist leaders in both the business and investment communities. This chapter begins with an explanation of several key complexities of our current energy production capabilities with regard to both carbon-based and alternative sources. It then examines the environmental strategies of Suncor, a major energy producer, and FedEx, a major energy user. The chapter concludes with the recounting of an exchange of letters between several major oil companies, a coalition of investors, and Ceres—a non-profit advocate for sustainable leadership. Through these communications, you will understand how the energy industry, in partnership with organizations like Ceres, can play a critical role in moving us toward a more sustainable future.

THE WHAT-IFS
OF OUR ENERGY FUTURE

As many analysts have recognized, carbon-based fuels such as oil and coal create two different categories of risk. First, continued dependence on burning fossil fuels is likely to bring about potentially devastating increases in global temperatures. Second, because energy companies represent trillions of dollars in assets, any abrupt decline in the value of those assets—such as what might be caused by drastic limitations on fossil fuel extraction—risks setting off a worldwide financial collapse. A 2014 Bloomberg white paper offers a snapshot of the scale of energy assets:

> Fossil fuel firms are a very large asset pool: $4.9trn in nearly 1,500 listed oil and gas companies, and a further $230bn in 275 coal companies. In addition to their public equity, these firms have issued hundreds of billions of dollars of debt. This massive scale is no surprise given that oil and gas firms are among the world's largest companies by equity value. ExxonMobil is the second-largest corporation in the world, after Apple, and nine of the ten largest oil and gas firms are worth more than $100bn each.

Meanwhile, alternative fuel sources, frequently touted as a solution to our energy ills, have barely made a dent in energy supply. Even with recent gains in electricity production through wind and solar power, as of 2013, only 13 percent of total U.S. electricity production was derived from alternative energy sources. And even that figure is misleading: One of the sources included in that number is hydroelectric power, but producing electricity from damming rivers is hardly a new technology. In fact, if you subtract the hydroelectric electricity production, less than 5 percent of our electricity comes from wind and solar power—what we classify as alternative sources. An anticipated 30 percent increase in world population over the next quarter century will render the transition to alternative energy sources all the more urgent.

TURBULENCE IN
THE CARBON-BASED FUEL INDUSTRY

In late 2014 and early 2015, oil companies faced an unanticipated challenge: the falling price of crude oil. Between 2009 and 2015, hydraulic fracturing (better known as "fracking") and horizontal drilling had increased U.S. oil production by nearly two-thirds. Although oil obtained by these means is much more expensive than oil produced through conventional drilling methods, the price of crude was sufficiently high enough to support the investments. But in June 2014, after having hovered near or above $100 a barrel for five years, prices began to slip; by early 2015, they had dropped sharply, to $50 a barrel, rendering unconventional drilling methods financially unsustainable.

Many energy companies that had relied on fracking suddenly found themselves having to suspend operations until the price of oil recovered or risk being forced out of business entirely. In the months following the price drop, though, fracking companies were able to rapidly develop new technology and streamline their operations so that they could remain competitive, even in the face of an extended downturn in oil prices.

In late 2014, the Organization of Petroleum Exporting Countries (OPEC) revealed that it had been a prime mover in the campaign to drive oil prices down. In fact, OPEC had committed to maintaining high levels of oil production precisely so that the price of oil would plummet. According to information released by Barclays and Commerzbank, OPEC's strategy was intended to force cutbacks in U.S. shale oil production.

Jamie Webster, an analyst at the investment management firm IHS, explained the situation this way: "The faster you bring the price down, the quicker you will have a response from U.S. production—that is the expectation and the hope. I cannot recall a time when several members [of OPEC] were actively pushing the price down in both word and deed." In other words, OPEC, seeking to maintain its long-term position as the key player in the oil market, was willing to endure short-term financial hardship in order to drive many of their competitors out of business.

Decline in oil prices is not the only threat to the fossil fuel industry. Another major risk can be summed up in the words "unburnable carbon." This was first introduced by the Carbon Tracker Initiative, a not-for-profit think tank aimed at enabling a climate-secure global energy market by aligning capital market actions with climate reality. This group predicts that at some point in the not-very-distant future, governments will be compelled to enact restrictive policies regarding carbon use. This would ensure that atmospheric carbon remains below the levels associated with a potentially disastrous rise in global temperatures. Some portion of the fossil fuels that form the asset base of energy companies will become off limits if we are to control the amount of carbon released into the atmosphere. This reserved portion is what is known as "unburnable carbon." According to a 2013 World Bank assessment, the amount of unburnable carbon the energy companies control could reduce the market value of conventional energy companies by 40 to 60 percent.

ALTERNATIVE ENERGY
CORPORATE RISKS AND SOCIAL REWARDS

Without question, alternative energy sources will be essential in addressing the looming threat of climate change. Yet energy production from renewable sources is not without drawbacks, and the associated costs are significant.

Unlike oil, natural gas, and coal, wind and solar power (currently the two principal alternative energy sources) are diffuse; that is, they require significant amounts of land in order to produce electricity. For instance, 17 acres are needed to produce 1 megawatt of electricity in the case of wind power, while 7.4 acres are required to produce a single megawatt using photovoltaic solar panels. Moreover, the installation of windmills, solar panels, and mirror collectors can disrupt or damage natural habitats.

Wind farms can also cause erosion in desert areas, and represent a serious danger to birds, which are often sucked into wind power generators. Finally, large-scale wind and solar farms require not only large tracts of land, but also the construction of roads, transformers, and transmission lines, which also impact the environment. Although the environmental consequences associated with alternative energy differ from those posed by carbon-based fuels, they are nonetheless serious, and should not be downplayed.

Wind and solar energy production face another potential hindrance: the scarcity of capital. Initially, most of the money invested in these technologies will consist of bonds and other securities issued by utilities or governments. Eventually, however, rapidly scaling up the use of alternative energy sources will require significant private investment as well. The Bloomberg white paper cited earlier on page 36 notes that "if fossil fuel divestment is to expand, the movement requires orders of magnitude more financial commitment." The report also warns, however, that attracting direct investment in clean energy assets may be difficult. Investors' concerns—such as a perceived lack of growth potential and the imposition of tariffs in some markets—are likely to lead to cautious "granular assessments" of the many factors that might influence potential returns. And in some cases, the report concludes, risks may simply seem too high, particularly for the institutional investor.

Despite the warnings, the Bloomberg report sees alternative energy as "a trillion-dollar investment opportunity for institutional investors." Tom Randall, a science writer and deputy sustainability editor at Bloomberg News, sums up the move toward more responsible energy production this way:

> Environmentalists see international climate talks . . . as key to containing climate change. But even without a sweeping agreement, the global shift toward cleaner fuels and more-efficient gadgets is underway.

In fact—and this goes back to the devaluation of conventional energy assets—failure to factor in the influence of new energy-generation technologies carries risk. As Nick Robins, the head of the HSBC Climate Change Centre, has warned: "There is this undertow of demand destruction going on through technological improvement. That's certainly not fully priced at the moment."

UNRECOGNIZED SOCIAL RESPONSE WARRIORS

Social response investors and environmental activists have shed important light on the consequences of the uncontrolled exploitation of carbon-based energy resources. Meanwhile, a number of new world companies—including Suncor and FedEx—are quietly leading the charge toward the responsible development, production, and use of energy resources.

Suncor
Innovation and Collaboration

Since its founding in 1917, Canadian energy giant Suncor has incorporated social response into its mission. The company's commitment to ESG principles has allowed it to enjoy some of the most rapid growth in the energy industry. Between 1999 and 2014, Suncor's market capitalization quadrupled—from $15 billion to more than $60 billion. To grow its business at this remarkable rate, Suncor focused on developing a large energy play in northern Alberta's Athabasca oil sands region. This area is home to the world's largest known reservoir of bitumen, an extremely dense form of crude oil. In the view of some observers, the oil produced in this region represents one of the most convincing arguments for completion of the Keystone XL Pipeline, which would facilitate the transportation of crude oil to U.S. refineries in Texas and Louisiana.

Suncor has demonstrated commitment to ESG standards through its choice of technologies, energy sources, and partnerships. As the developer (and first adopter) of the Tailings Reduction Operations Method (TROTM), Suncor became the leader in the capture and disposal of *tailings*. Tailings consist of the clay, silt, sand, bitumen, and water that remain after the bitumen is extracted from the sand. Under the TROTM approach, the waste stream is piped into ponds, where most of the solids settle to the bottom; meanwhile, the waste water evaporates or is reused in the reclamation process.

The key benefit of the technology is that it significantly shortens the time between the capture and isolation of the mining waste and the restoration of the land to pristine wilderness. Suncor has been so successful in achieving rapid environmental restoration that it has been able to eliminate the need for at least five tailings

Flex
In the Energy Industry

Flex (formerly Flextronics), the behind-the-scenes new world company mentioned in the Introduction, is involved in the manufacture of products that support businesses in many different industries. So many industries, in fact, that without this company, world economic growth might not have reached the levels it has over the past several decades. This is especially true of the energy industry.

Among Flex's numerous products are photovoltaic (PV) modules—interconnected groups of solar cells that capture the sun's energy and are components of solar energy panels. Flex has manufactured and delivered millions of these PV modules to solar energy companies throughout the world.

Flex's supply chain, which is managed with a focus on being as efficient and economical as possible, contributes to the reduction of carbon emissions into the atmosphere. The company's influence is global, supporting the development of solar and wind energy power solutions in the United States, Canada, Mexico, and Brazil, as well as countries throughout Europe and Asia.

ponds at its mining sites. The company anticipates reducing the total number of tailings ponds from eight to two in the near future, further reducing environmental impact by decreasing the amount of land needed for reclamation activities.

In addition to employing responsible energy extraction and environmental restoration practices, Suncor has allotted resources for the development of alternative energy sources, including wind power. But perhaps the most important of Suncor's contributions to sustainable energy is its role in the establishment of Canada's

Oil Sands Innovation Alliance (COSIA). This partnership is dedicated to developing and implementing technologies that support a toxin-free environment in oil sands extraction areas. In its focus on improving environmental performance through collaboration and innovation, COSIA has facilitated faster movement along the innovation curve. By 2014, the group's thirteen members had created a pool of intellectual property—including the knowledge of how to effectively extract oil resources—worth over $1 billion. It has engaged in numerous joint projects to reduce environmental impact. Shell, for example, another COSIA member, has developed its own reclamation process called Atmospheric Fines Drying (AFD). This process allows water to be rapidly extracted from tailings, thereby speeding up the restoration of the natural habitat.

In every one of its efforts to reduce the environmental impact of its operations, Suncor has revealed a sense of respect for the landscape, for nearby settlements, and for the broader world of consumers who depend on the energy produced by the firm. In turn, this respect has not only bolstered the firm's reputation, both within and outside the energy community, it has also enabled Suncor to achieve greater financial returns. Thus, while helping its industry realize gains in the realm of environmental protection, Suncor has successfully translated "sustainable value" into numbers that speak to the financial community.

FedEx
Working Globally, Acting Efficiently

While Suncor has been instrumental in directly improving its sustainability, efficiency, and financial performance with regard to energy and environmental resources, FedEx—another new world firm—has been a champion of sustainable environmental practices in a less direct, but no less impactful way.

Federal Express officially began operations on April 17, 1973, with 389 team members. That night, fourteen small aircraft took off from Memphis, Tennessee, and delivered 186 packages to twenty-five U.S. cities from Rochester, New York, to Miami, Florida. Today, FedEx Corporation has more than 325,000 team members worldwide and delivers over 9 million shipments a day in 220 countries and territories. Thanks to the company's portfolio of services, FedEx customers can ship to "every address in the United States."

With a worldwide delivery system that makes use of nearly 650 aircraft, the company saw an opportunity to lead the way in the realm of transportation-related energy efficiency by zeroing in on jet aircraft design. At a time when most people believed that jets had reached their peak efficiency, FedEx teamed with Boeing to introduce the Boeing 777 freighter, an aircraft with 18 percent fewer emissions than the MD-11. In introducing the Boeing 777, FedEx and Boeing did for air cargo transportation what Toyota has done for automobile travel. They made it not only more efficient and environmentally friendly, but also more socially responsive.

Thanks to the design of the 777, formerly inefficient flights between remote regions became faster and less costly. Planes flying between the United States and Asia, for example, no longer had to stop in Alaska to refuel, and the flight time was cut by two hours. Such efficiency innovations as the Boeing 777 have allowed FedEx to continuously broaden its global reach, bringing international locations into the fold more efficiently, and supporting economic growth in the most remote regions of the planet. In the process, FedEx uses less fuel for flights to/from Asia and creates fewer toxic emissions than had previously been possible.

Along with its breakthrough contributions to aircraft technology, FedEx has developed digitally based alternatives to physical shipping and delivery (i.e. dematerialized deliveries). These alternatives have resulted in breakthroughs in efficiency while addressing the demands of the exponential increases in the volume and range of its deliveries.

In the words of FedEx founder, chairman, and CEO Fred Smith, "The information about the package is as important as the package itself." The "information" he is referring to is data. Access to such data is readily available in the digital age. To explain, it is important to begin with the 800 MHz (megahertz) spectrum. This spectrum is the part of the digital bandwidth that had been reserved for television broadcasts. Recently, it has been re-allocated for use in digital communications. In 1980, FedEx began buying up the 800MHz spectrum across the United States and Canada. Why? The company had already recognized the key role that data would play in business success, and that a rapid, wireless communications infrastructure was needed to support that role. Thanks to this extraordinary foresight, decades later FedEx is still at the forefront of digital collection and dissemination of delivery information.

In what may be its most extraordinary innovation, FedEx has developed a carbon-neutral aspect to its FedEx envelope shipping service: FedEx Express makes investments in global projects that displace or sequester greenhouse gas emissions from the atmosphere, neutralizing the impacts of carbon emissions emitted during the shipment of all FedEx envelopes around the world.

In a recent interview, Mitch Jackson, vice president of environmental affairs and sustainability at FedEx, explained that when he was charged with strengthening the company's sustainability culture, he looked to align the FedEx Sustainability Program to how it runs its business—by focusing on what matters to the company, its customers, its team members, and its shareowners. In Jackson's view, Toyota's history is an example that big-picture issues like sustainability are the keys to growth. Toyota executives, Jackson said, looked through a "lens of sustainability" to develop their long-term vision for the company. By asking what the role of personal transportation would be in the lives of people around the world, Jackson felt that Toyota had changed the focus of its business.

Jackson views Toyota as a true pioneer in the realm of aligning sustainability with organizational purpose. In Jackson's view, "the romance of global capitalism" is rarely perceived to be in sync with sustainable strategies. But FedEx doesn't subscribe to that perspective. According to Jackson, in turbulent times, the engines of success include "hatred of waste," logistical efficiency, and providing relevant solutions for different markets. According to Jackson, too many corporations fail to see that applied sustainability is not one-size-fits-all: different geographic and market segments require unique strategies and approaches. He outlines his view of his company's commitment to ESG values through its focus in four areas—technical and operational performance, transparency, innovation, and leadership—as shown in Figure 2.1 on page 47.

Performance is the company's first area of focus—it is the primary level at which all firms compete. In the case of FedEx and other delivery giants, this involves company logistics—such as the performance of the trucks and jets, the loading and unloading of packages, and the skill and training of navigators.

As a new world company, FedEx expands its scope of impact and influence to include *transparency*, both within its corporate entity and without into suppliers and society at large. It is why they publish an annual citizenship report.

Continuing to the next level, *innovation* refers to "classic" innovation that involves advancing the norms. One example is FedEx's teaming with Boeing to develop the long-haul Boeing 777 freighter, with a longer range and lower emissions.

The final area of FedEx's focus as a new world company is *leadership*. Basically, this means becoming a leader in social solutions—

even before the problems become apparent. It is like fixing the traffic problems for an entire city before the town leaders even know how to ask for it. FedEx leads in a world where information is as valuable as the delivered package, something that companies like Amazon grew from as well.

In essence, FedEx is a social response giant that brings these four areas of sustainability focus into a consistent alignment in function and purpose. FedEx does not just deliver packages. It connects entrepreneurs, product developers, and manufacturers with key partners all over the world. As Mitch Jackson put it, FedEx's role is "to connect the world responsibly and resourcefully."

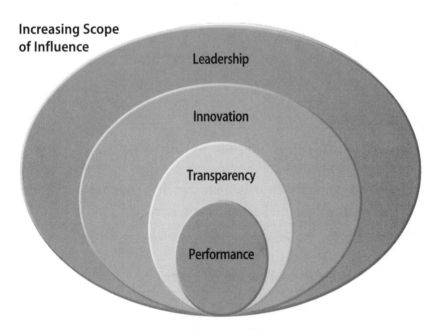

Figure 2.1. Practical Sustainability

This figure summarizes FedEx's commitment to ESG values through its focus in four areas—technical performance (company logistics), transparency (disclosure of business practices), innovation (advancing the norms), and leadership (focus on social/policy-driven solutions).

ACTIVIST INVESTORS AT THE NEW ENERGY FRONTIER

In the wake of the 1989 Exxon Valdez oil spill, which dumped 10.8 million gallons of crude into Alaska's Prince William Sound, a small group of investors joined together to found Ceres, a non-profit organization with the goal to "forge a new sustainable business model, one that would protect the health of the planet and the long-term prosperity of its people." The Ceres coalition includes more than 130 investors, environmental groups, and public interest organizations. Its motto, "Mobilizing Business Leadership for a Sustainable World," reveals a great deal about how Ceres works. Through its unique position "at the nexus of the business, investment and advocacy communities," Ceres leverages "the power of . . . leading investors, Fortune 500 companies, thought leaders and policymakers—to positively influence change."

Ceres' purpose at the time of its founding can best be characterized this way: to create a narrow but reliable avenue for shareholder influence on a company's choices—from product development, to manufacturing and distribution, to long-term growth strategies. In the intervening years, however, growing awareness of what ESG standards mean to investors, customers, and clients has widened what was once a narrow avenue into a superhighway.

The Ceres Letter

The April 2010 Deepwater Horizon disaster, also referred to as the BP oil spill, pumped more than 3 million barrels of oil (over 130 million gallons) into the Gulf of Mexico; years later, the full environmental impact remains unknown. In August of 2010, on behalf of more than fifty oil-company investors, Ceres sent a letter to the major oil companies, encouraging them to reassure their investors that they had adequate measures in place to prevent future spills, and to respond should those measures fail.

Just over three years later, Mindy Lubber, president of Ceres and director of its Investor Network on Climate Risk (INCR), sent a significantly more assertive letter to forty-five of the world's largest energy companies. The letter was written on behalf of seventy leading global investment management organizations that control more than $3 trillion in assets. It focused on two key questions: "What steps are the energy companies taking to develop sufficient alternative energy sources to reduce fossil fuel use by approximately 80 percent by mid-century?" and "In the face of likely global policies limiting the exploitation of carbon-based fuels and the issue of unburnable carbon, how are the energy companies planning to protect investor interests?"

The letter closed by asking the companies to respond to the participating investors who had signed the letter. They were asked to let the investors know of their commitment to managing the risks delineated in the letter, and of the role their Board of Directors would play in overseeing their assessment of risk.

The 2013 letter demonstrated how much more influential ESG investors had become in the intervening three years. It also crystallized Ceres' position as one of the most—if not *the* most—prominent and important voices in the expanding ESG universe.

The Corporate Response

Many of the companies that received the Ceres letter chose not to acknowledge it; several, however—including Statoil, Norway's largest oil company, and ExxonMobil—did respond.

In her response, Hilde Merete Nafstad, Statoil's senior vice president for investor relations, described the company as being "deeply concerned with the challenge of climate change," with respect to both its environmental impact and its impact on the energy industry. In support of this statement, Nafstad declared Statoil's support for the goal of the United Nations Framework Convention on Climate Change, which is to "prevent dangerous anthropogenic (i.e., human) interference of the climate system," and acknowledged that "limiting energy related greenhouse gas . . . emissions is an important element" in that effort. Finally, the letter declared Statoil's agreement with the findings of what was then the most recent report from the Intergovernmental Panel on

The Kyoto Protocol

The Kyoto Protocol is a written agreement regarding the amount of potentially damaging carbon emissions in the environment. It was created by the United Nations Framework Convention on Climate Change (UNFCCC) and adopted in Kyoto, Japan, in 1997.

The protocol's first "commitment period"—the time when the required restrictions were to be followed by nations that had signed the agreement—lasted until 2012. A second commitment period was set to last from January 1, 2013, through December 31, 2020. This new agreement contained a revised list of greenhouse gases (GHG), as well as additions and modifications to a number of terms of the original. Thirty-seven industrialized nations signed the first Kyoto Protocol. The United States was not among them. And many of the developed countries that did sign have not honored their commitments to reduce the carbon released into the atmosphere.

The new world companies discussed in this book have, in effect, taken the responsibility to support the carbon-reduction standards of the Kyoto Protocol on their own, doing for our planet what many nations are failing to do.

Climate Change (IPCC), as well as its support for both the first and second phases of the Kyoto Protocol (see the inset on page 50).

One important aspect of the Statoil response is its clarification of the distinction between the definition of *reserves* used by commercial energy companies and the definition used by the International Energy Association (IEA) and other regulatory agencies. According to Nafstad's letter, "publicly listed oil and gas companies" use "reserves" to refer to "a quantity of oil and gas that is close to investment decision for development and production." Regulatory agencies, however, use the term more broadly; the IEA, for example, bases its definition of reserves on the "total potential emissions from fossil fuel reserves in 2012." Thus, in practical terms, most of what the IEA calls "reserves" would be classified as "resources" by oil and gas companies and would not be incorporated into the companies' calculations of available reserves. Statoil's letter explained that because of the distinction in the use of terminology, the firm's estimate of exploitable reserves is only about one-third that of the IEA. This variation in defining the word "reserves" turns out to be highly problematic.

To further explain, as Nafstad points out, on a worldwide basis, as much as two-thirds of the "carbon reserves" identified by the IEA are from coal, whereas only "22 percent are from oil and 15 percent from natural gas, respectively." The problem is that the IEA uses total potential emissions as the basis of its calculations in determining available reserves, while oil and gas companies use the physical amounts of coal, oil, and gas in their calculations of reserves. In fact, CO_2 emissions from coal are much greater than those from other fossil fuel sources. This means that, while actual physical coal reserves are very small and do not generate nearly the energy equivalents of oil and gas reserves, the IEA's calculations significantly over-represent physical coal as a percentage of all reserves.

The letter further describes Statoil's strategic decisions and likens them to those of other energy companies:

> [They] will continue to be based on expected risk-weighted returns; where costs, prices and relevant strategic elements (such as policy, subsurface uncertainties and proximity to infrastructure and markets) are taken into consideration. In recent years the issue of climate change and possible climate policy regulations are indeed incorporated into such decisions.

Observing that "stronger regulatory requirements in the future" are likely to increase carbon costs, Nafstad emphasizes the company's commitment to "carbon efficiency" and its associated "competitive advantage." The letter cites the company's progress in developing "carbon capture and storage" on two of its oil fields, as well as its ongoing research into new ways to use this strategy. Also included is the following overview of how the company plans to proceed:

> Ultimately, a stricter climate policy will imply lower demand for oil and gas and lower prices. This goes directly to the economic robustness of the project portfolio of the oil and gas industry, and adds a significant uncertainty that must be actively managed. In Statoil, we are of the opinion that we have a fairly robust project portfolio, even in the event that global or regional climate regulations were to become much stricter than what we currently expect.

In other words, Statoil is confident that it is on the right path with respect to protecting both the climate and the interests of its investors.

In stark contrast to Statoil, which had explicitly aligned itself with the positions of both the United Nations and the IPCC,

ExxonMobil's response to the Ceres letter states flatly that "We do not sign on to other people's principles." But these words are at odds with statements elsewhere in the letter, which indicate that ExxonMobil is aware of the risks associated with climate change and is taking steps to deal with the consequences as they relate to conventional oil and gas exploration and production.

Many details of ExxonMobil's response to the Ceres letter are incorporated by reference to various sections of a 2014 company report titled *Energy and Carbon: Managing the Risks.* Notably, the energy production and risk management principles outlined in that document are similar to those described in Statoil's response.

As part of a thirty-year energy outlook (through 2040), the ExxonMobil report predicts a global population increase of 2 billion, but also anticipates worldwide gains in gross domestic product that will "outpace population gains . . . resulting in higher living standards." The report projects a 35-percent increase in world energy demand by 2040, and notes that a combination of increased efficiency and the wider use of less carbon-dependent fuels will be needed to meet the demand.

In a section titled "Carbon Budget and Carbon Asset Risk Implications," the report offers a "low carbon scenario" in which the cost of reducing the level of CO_2 from 650 parts per million (ppm) to the 450 ppm necessary to avoid climate disaster is estimated at $200 per ton. At the time the report was written, ExxonMobil estimated that the cost of emitting a ton of CO_2 into the atmosphere was "approximately $8 to $10." The report also cites an IEA estimate that the cost of reducing carbon emissions to "50 percent below 2005 levels by 2050 would require $45 trillion in added energy and infrastructure investments."

Figure 2.2 on page 54 represents ExxonMobil's estimate of the *proxy cost* of climate risk in assessing the cost of energy. This method of determining the cost of energy is not based on existing

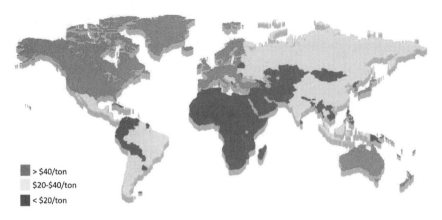

Figure 2.2 Increasing Focus on Climate Risk

This figure represents what ExxonMobil anticipates as the future energy costs in countries throughout the world. Due to various factors—such as the availability of unexploited energy resources and the differing value of currencies—the relative costs of extracting energy are much higher in countries like the United States and Australia than they are, for instance, in China.

data but on the anticipated costs. It is often used when data is not available, such as, in this case, for a future projection. This figure shows significant differences in the projected future energy costs for different countries.

Meeting growing energy demand while achieving these reductions in CO_2 levels would require massive installation of new nuclear plants, coal plants outfitted with carbon capture and sequestration facilities, and between 3,700 and 17,800 wind turbines, each with a four-megawatt production capacity.

Like Statoil, ExxonMobil embraces environmentally responsible practices. According to its standards of business conduct, ExxonMobil is committed to complying with "all applicable environmental laws and regulations," and to the application of "responsible standards" in the absence of such laws and regulations. The company promotes "appropriate operating practices and training" to encourage "concern and respect for the environment." Finally, ExxonMobil pledges to "respond quickly and effectively" to accidents that occur at its sites, and to engage in research "to improve understanding of the impact of its business on the environment . . . and to enhance its capability to make operations and products compatible with the environment."

Based on my reviews of the policy statements and annual reports of many other energy companies, it is clear that Statoil and ExxonMobil are not alone in their support of the values held by and the outcomes sought by the ESG community. The disagreements center on the energy fundamentals upon which company policies and practices are based. I believe, however, that these differences can be overcome as we discover precisely what they are, and find ways to become partners rather than adversaries.

New world companies feel obligated to build bridges between themselves and their customers and clients. Figure 2.3 on page 56 presents ExxonMobil's projected breakdown of the real world prices that CO_2 restriction options are expected to cost their customers in the coming years. (Figures are based on median U.S. income, which would obviously vary across demographics.) Not surprising, the more carbon that is released into the atmosphere, the greater the monetary cost.

According to its standards of business conduct, ExxonMobil is committed to complying with "all applicable environmental laws and regulations" and to the application of "responsible standards" in the absence of such laws and regulations. Yet something more social is happening in these Exxon exhibits.

The company promotes "appropriate operating practices and training" to encourage "concern and respect for the environment." Finally, ExxonMobil pledges to "respond quickly and effectively" to accidents that occur at its sites, and to engage in research "to improve understanding of the impact of its business on the environment . . . and to enhance its capability to make operations and products compatible with the environment."

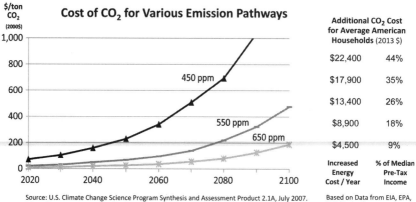

Figure 2.3. Projected Costs of Restricting CO_2 Emissions

This chart presents ExxonMobil's projected future costs of reducing carbon emissions for the average American household. As the chart indicates, the more carbon that is released, the greater the monetary cost. To serve as an example, it shows that the projected cost of reducing the carbon level to 650 ppm (parts per million) is $4,500.00 per American household through the year 2100. If that level is significantly reduced to 450 ppm, that cost would escalate dramatically to $22,400.00 by 2085.

Siemens
Addressing Important Energy Issues

Siemens AG is a global technology company with a strong specialization in the energy industry. Formed over a century and a half ago, the company employs some 343,000 people in more than 200 countries and generated $98 billion in revenues worldwide in 2014. In the U.S. and Puerto Rico, Siemens has over 46,000 employees and generated more than $22 billion in revenues during the same time period.

Siemens is a worldwide pioneer in clean and efficient energy production, with four of its divisions—Power and Gas, Wind Power and Renewables, Power Generation Services, and Energy Management—focusing in this area. Its Power and Gas division and Power Generation Services division concentrate on meeting present global energy needs. At the same time, through its Wind Power and Renewables and Energy Management divisions, the company looks toward the future as it integrates new non-fossil-fuel technologies into its corporate activities. Its Power and Gas division partners with power company customers in the United States to help them operate fossil power plants and to meet economic and ecological challenges specific to the American market.

The company's portfolio is focused on addressing the growing challenges of climate change through the production, installation, and management of the following:

- Gas and steam turbines for power plants.

- Production generators and compressors targeted to oil and natural gas production and transport.

- Gas-fired power plant solutions.

- Power and process automation solutions for industrial clients.

Across the United States, Siemens' power and gas solutions are helping ensure reliable and efficient power production. Among the company's innovations is the *tri-generation system*—a combined cooling, heating, and power generation scheme. In New York, for example, the Riverbay tri-generation scheme provides power for around 60,000 residents in the Bronx. Thanks to combined cycle power plant technology, a reliable power supply is guaranteed to inhabitants in the area.

Through its Wind Power and Renewables division, Siemens has more than 25,000 megawatts of wind-generated power installations in operation. Its platform strategy includes both onshore and offshore wind power plants. With its first offshore wind power plant installed in Denmark in 1991, Siemens can be considered the "founding father" of this industry. In addition, it is installing over 400 wind power plants in the state of Iowa with an estimated power output of more than 1,000 megawatts. This division is also responsible for the installation of hydropower plants, including sub-surface ocean plants that capture energy from tides and currents. The company's energy management division also manages the efficient transmission of large volumes of energy to enhance the power exchange between power grids.

Siemens characterizes itself as a Totally Integrated Power (TIP) provider for electrical solutions because of the broad spectrum of energy production and management services it provides. It is truly what I consider the epitome of a new world company.

CONCLUSION

The website of Wintershall, a German energy firm, sums up our reliance on fossil fuels this way:

> Life without oil? Impossible! . . . 40 percent of all textiles contain oil . . . 40 billion liters of oil a year are used to make CDs and DVDs. . . . A single sofa contains 60 liters of oil. Modern life is inconceivable without crude oil. The world consumes almost 14 billion liters of oil each day.

I would make a single important change to these words: instead of "Impossible!" I would say "Currently impossible." Today, our use of carbon-based fuels is the single greatest threat to our environment and, ultimately, to the survival of the planet. And unless we find sustainable ways to address our energy needs, little of what we do in the social and governance realms will ultimately matter. But as companies around the world embrace and implement the principles of social response capitalism, the move to replace carbon-based fuels will gather force, and carry us toward what I call a *renewable future*.

New world companies are organizations that not only identify social needs, but also find a way to meet them, often by working in tandem with other new world companies. For example, FedEx's Mitch Jackson was instrumental in establishing a renewable energy partnership with the global energy company BP. Under this arrangement, BP researches locations where it makes sense to develop renewable energy resources. By investing with BP to develop carbon-neutral energy sources, FedEx is offsetting its use of carbon-intensive modes of transportation.

In addition, the call for research into renewable energy sources by the U.S. government is getting stronger, and it is being led by prominent business leaders. The American Energy Innovation Council is made up of six prominent business leaders, including Microsoft's Bill Gates and General Electric's Jeffrey Immelt. They make the case that the United States is spending a much lower percentage of its Gross Domestic Product on this sort of research than many other countries, including China, Japan, and France. Joseph J. Romm, who worked on federal energy research during the Clinton administration, has a tempered view of the government's role: "I am 100 percent for more research, since who could possibly oppose that?" he said, following that comment with a qualification: "But it is only a small part of the answer, and certainly not the most important."

At the same time, though, many investors are increasingly divesting their portfolios of oil and gas. Most recently, Rockefeller heirs, controlling some $860 billion in assets, closed their positions in fossil fuel investments. They are part of a broad coalition of some 800 million global investors who plan to withdraw $50 billion in carbon-based energy investments over a five-year period.

The movement is continuing from another direction as well. A February 2015 poll of nearly 3,000 Americans revealed that 66 percent of those polled believed it was the government's moral obligation to reduce CO_2 emissions in order to avoid the damage that might result from global warming. Nearly three quarters of those responding said that they themselves felt a moral obligation to work toward CO_2 reduction.

The work of social response investors and environmental activists has shed important light on the consequences of the uncontrolled exploitation of carbon-based energy resources. This is leading us to the very solutions investors see as important keys to our future energy sustainability.

This chapter provides a framework of hope—a lattice on which to grow our new social expectations and values that answer our global energy transformation. This movement is the beginning of a needed middle narrative that seeks a reliable world where energy matters more than money. It is a framework that will be tested by the great storms ahead in the world markets; but, a set of sensible energy solutions shall, after continual rebuffs, prevail.

3

A Merger of Metrics

Managing the Near Future

One of the keys to assessing the value of a company is the likelihood that it will remain not simply *viable* but *highly competitive* even decades into the future. More and more the evidence is indicating that the degree to which a company follows and advances the principles embodied in environmental, social, and governance metrics is a reliable indicator of its long-term success. One of the reasons is that these measures assess long-range outcomes to a much greater degree than analytics that focus almost exclusively on short-term quarterly and annual financial performances.

This chapter provides an overview of what I call the "people principles" in modern capitalism, otherwise known as the social and governance metrics. Both focus on the people involved in the way businesses conduct themselves, but from different points of view. The governance metric centers itself on the people who run the corporations, while the social metric focuses on the people who work for the companies, as well as those who buy their products and services. The social metric also includes people whose lives are indirectly affected—for better or worse—by the way in which the companies do business.

Although the people affected by the social and governance measures may seem to hold very different perspectives regarding how they view individual corporations; in fact, what amounts to a point-of-view merger has been taking place over the past several decades. This change has been brought about as new technology creates a much more unified and connected global business world, a world in which customers and clients often have a growing voice in corporate policies and practices. In some cases, their voices are as strong as those of the executives that oversee the businesses.

This is not to say that executives don't run companies any more. Rather, it is to say that the definition of "run" has lost its sense of exclusivity and privilege, and has become something that is now much more inclusive of people throughout the corporation, as well as the general public. Companies are becoming much more reflective of how these two groups of people see and influence corporate policies and practices.

This transformation is taking place as a growing number of board members and executive teams are realizing their need to be aware of and respond to ESG trends. Corporate leaders are still very well compensated for making informed decisions on how their firms can and should compete in the marketplace, but the issue of executive compensation is increasingly entering into the ESG debate. And as they work to make intelligent, balanced decisions for their companies, they also understand the need to incorporate the concerns of their employees and the public into decisions regarding such diverse ESG issues as:

- The role of racial and gender diversity in their boards of directors, employees, and customers.

- Their own roles and compensation as corporate officers.

- Equal opportunity policies.

- The influence of environmental issues such as carbon policy on climate change, and how the company can address the potential negative consequences of their impact on the earth.

- The importance of adequate as well as continuous training for employees.

- Corporate health and safety policies, including the coverage of lost time by employees suffering from accidents, illnesses, or due to pregnancies.

At the same time, the increasing availability of ESG data is helping investors and analysts look into corporations with greater accuracy and transparency. Through this criteria, they are able to determine how well companies are responding to a rapidly changing global business environment.

THE EMERGENCE OF
SOCIAL AND GOVERNANCE METRICS

A company's integration of social and governance metrics can have a great and positive impact on a large and varied group of people. These measures affect corporate officers and how they conduct company business; employees—how they are treated and how much responsibility they are given in the new world corporate environment; clients and customers, who purchase a company's products and services; and finally, the citizens of the planet. This subtle transition has been going on for decades.

In 1970, consumer advocate Ralph Nader initiated one of the first such public actions. With the Project for Corporate Responsibility, a group of young attorneys associated with Nader, submitted nine social issue proposals to General Motors prior to the company's annual shareholder meeting. Among the issues proposed included race and gender equality, environmental activism, and the creation of a Committee for Corporate Responsibility. Membership for the committee was to be chosen collectively by a member of the GM Board of Directors, the Project for Corporate Responsibility, and the United Auto Workers.

GM reacted strongly against the proposals. It did, however, reluctantly put up two of the proposals for shareholder vote, which failed to pass. Despite its initial negative reaction, GM did implement some of the actions recommended, which included the creation of a public policy committee and the inclusion of an African American, the Reverend Leon Sullivan, as a member of its board. In the two decades following this approach to GM, consumer awareness of social responsibility began to make significant inroads as a factor in choosing one product over another.

In a paper presented by the Center for Ethical Business Cultures, the evolution of social and governance issues is described in this way:

> Some issues, such as animal rights, military contracting, and engagement in South Africa declined in importance, while resolutions concerning tobacco, labor, corporate political activity, and governance (including compensation) became more frequent toward the end of the 1990s.

As that trend evolved, consumer power began to increase in proportion to the growth of information provided by the Internet. As the Internet rapidly became our primary tool for the sharing and acquisition of insights on firms, the need for companies to take social values into consideration began to play an ever more important role in the way they did business. This birthed social response capitalism.

These developments marked significant milestones in the acceptance of social and governance metrics as key components of corporate policy. Early stages of this evolution focused on such specific issues as whether or not to do business with the racially segregated apartheid nation of South Africa. In the 1980s and '90s, areas of concern expanded to include health and employment issues for workers, compensation for board members and executives, and corporate involvement in political activity.

As I see it, the 2008 financial collapse—what I call "the big chill of 2008"—happened in no small part because a number of major companies had not adopted the policies and practices of social response capitalism. Instead of translating concern for social and governance issues into corporate action, which would very likely have created a much more socially responsible and ethical environment, what emerged was a new kind of speculative capitalism. The next chapter provides an in-depth look at speculative capitalism and the dangerous financial environment that results. It also shows how new world companies—with their increased adherence to ESG principles—are coming to the rescue. This is a battle of significant social impact.

PARTNERING WITH OTHER COMPANIES

There are a number of ways to analyze the degree to which social and governance metrics influence a company's practice of social response capitalism. Among them is through its business relationships, from its partners to its suppliers. Before partnering with other businesses, companies need to consider if they share the same social and governance perspectives. Are the companies charitable? Do they support worthwhile causes for the betterment of local communities and the world at large? Are they concerned with employee health and safety? Are their shareholders' interests in furthering social and governance performance given strong consideration?

The catalog of social metrics criteria focuses on a company's attention to the welfare of its employees. It tracks areas such as how much time an employee loses due to an accident, how much time the company devotes to training its employees, whether it follows equal opportunity employment standards, and whether it spends at least 1 percent of its pre-tax profits on projects that benefit the communities in which it is located. In addition, the social metric involves listening to the collective voice of its customers and paying attention to the consequences of its corporate policies on the people in its corporate neighborhood and around the world. Of course, all this is done without losing sight of a company's profitability.

THE EVOLVING GOVERNANCE
AND SOCIAL METRICS

The new—and in my view, the more fundamentally sound—social response capitalism is based on a commitment by companies to broaden their exclusive focus on the bottom line to include quality, social response, and price. It should also add significant changes to the way corporate governance is carried out. Through these valued changes, a corporation can measure its own progress toward achieving new world company status.

The Deming View

One of the early advocates for this new "leadership capitalism" was business analyst Dr. William Edwards Deming, whose redefinition of capitalism is based on governance metrics. In his 1982 book, *Out of Crisis*, Deming asserted that the modern corporation must compete not only on price, but also on quality. In his famous "14 Points for Management," he laid out exactly what corporations must do in order to transform themselves from objective-based companies to leadership-based companies. He explained how bottom-line focus must expand to address more important and ultimately more rewarding leadership-based management changes centered on social responsibility. I won't present all of Deming's points here, but I do want to summarize what I see as the most important elements of his game-changing list of business practices.

Deming recognized that "we are in a new economic age." In order to meet the challenges of the new business reality, corporations need to improve "quality and productivity." One of the ways he felt this could be done was by changing the concept of "leadership." No longer should it refer to a top-down, upper management-driven practice. Rather, it should be achieved through the distribution of leadership responsibilities to those at all levels in a corporation.

Deming also emphasized the need to "break down barriers between departments." This would make people in every critical area of the company, from research and development to "design, sales, and production," work together as a team. He emphasized getting rid of "targets" and "numerical goals" for measuring performance, which he felt created "adversarial relationships" among employees who should be, above all, team members working toward the same goals. Breaking down these barriers would enable them to experience "pride of workmanship" and let them understand that every employee is part of a team working to achieve "transformation." In Deming's words, "The transformation is everybody's job."

The governance metric is one that is evolving rapidly. In new world companies, the "leadership team" is proving ever more valuable than the increasingly obsolete cult of the CEO, which had long been the key focus of an analyst's corporate evaluations. Good governance now demands a much more balanced and team-based approach to running a firm, with greater focus on the functions of leadership teams.

With regard to governance, "investors want to know that a company uses accurate and transparent accounting methods, and they want to see that common stockholders are allowed to vote on important issues. They also want companies to avoid conflicts of interest in their choice of board members. Finally, they prefer not to invest in companies that engage in illegal behavior or use political contributions to obtain favorable treatment."

The governance metric as articulated by Deming focuses directly on a company's treatment of employees, integrating them into decision-making processes and giving them more responsibility. In effect, this approach is an effort to "democratize" the company's governance strategy. Since the publication of Deming's book, however, the treatment of employees falls more under the social metric. Today, the governance metric tends to focus more on corporate structure and practices, while the social metric involves a company's employees, its customers, and the impact it has on society at large. The ESG lens blends all of these factors to reduce risk in the firm.

Reuters' Vision

Thomson Reuters, one of the world's major sources of information for businesses, has been instrumental in advancing focus on the social metric. The company was created in 2008 when the Thomson Corporation, a Toronto-based media and information company, purchased the Reuters Group. With more than 60,000 employees worldwide, Thomson Reuters is one of the largest media companies in the world. Its description of the "social pillar" indicates just how far the combining of social and governance principles has come:

> The social pillar measures a company's capacity to generate trust and loyalty with its workforce, customers and society, through its use of best management practices. It is a reflection of the company's reputation and the health of its license to operate, which are key factors in determining its ability to generate long-term shareholder value.

In an important sense, Thomson Reuters expanded the social component of governance into the social metric further than Governance Metrics International (GMI) had. GMI, discussed on page 72, described the focus of the governance metric almost exclusively on corporate management and executive behavior.

ANALYZING ESG METRICS

While understanding the principles of social response capitalism is essential, it is equally important to be able to measure the degree to which these principles are put into practice. And then from such measurements, open and accurate investment conclusions can be drawn. To do this, a number of tools have been made available to both corporations and the public. Among them are The Bloomberg BCAUSE Impact Report and Governance Metrics International Ratings.

The Bloomberg BCAUSE Impact Report

In response to what it saw as a growing need for governance changes, the financial analytics firm Bloomberg launched its ESG Data Service in 2009. In doing so, the company furthered the legitimacy of ESG analytics as important predictors of corporate success. One publication that advances the ESG cause is the Bloomberg sustainability report, which has been renamed The Bloomberg BCAUSE Impact Report. Published annually, this report has effectively defined the components of both social and governance metrics.

The governance criteria tracked in this report range from the size of a company's board of directors to its compliance with the United Nations' Principles for Responsible Investment (PRI) and the Global Reporting Initiative (GRI). This report also tracks the percentage of women on the company's board of directors, the number of board meetings held annually, and whether executive compensation is linked to meeting the company's ESG goals.

The transition from exclusive top-down executive management to management that is more evenly distributed down the chain of authority is a significant move toward social response capitalism. I have often referred to "corporate mansions" when describing old-style corporations in which top executives exercise absolute control over the decisions made at every corporate level. Now, as ESG metrics are becoming more important to a company's success and as authority is distributed more equitably throughout the corporation, these companies can be better described as "corporate ranch houses." The sense of exclusive executive entitlement has given way to an organizational model in which more key personnel are occupying (metaphorically at least) the same level in the corporate home.

Governance Metrics International (GMI) Ratings

Another important group that tracks ESG metrics is Governance Metrics International (GMI) Ratings. A division of Morgan Stanley Capital International, GMI Ratings:

> . . . is a pioneer in the application of non-traditional risk metrics to investment analysis and risk modeling. Formed in 2010 through the merger of The Corporate Library, Governance Metrics International, and Audit Integrity, GMI Ratings provides global research coverage of the environmental, social, governance and accounting-related risks affecting the performance of public companies. GMI Ratings is a signatory to the United Nations-backed Principles for Responsible Investment (PRI).

GMI Ratings covers a wide variety of governance metrics through its reports, which include the following:

■ Accounting and Governance Risk (AGR) 50 Lists

This rating uses a proven quantitative, statistical process to identify accounting items associated with fraudulent financial statements, as well as governance characteristics associated with firms that have been prosecuted for accounting fraud. As a group, companies with very low AGR ratings have an elevated risk of enforcement action for accounting fraud, have greater market price volatility, and are more likely to experience severe price drops.

■ Governance Insight Alerts

These alerts involve "in-depth research, ratings and analysis of the environmental, social, and governance-related business practices of thousands of companies worldwide." They are designed to alert investors to risks associated with ESG values and practices that they might not find in conventional investment analyses.

■ CEO Pay Surveys

Published periodically, this survey considers 2,259 CEOs whose tenure spanned the whole of the last two years in order to determine changes in executive compensation from 2011 to 2012.

■ "Golden Parachute" Report

In 2014, GMI Ratings released this report identifying the largest severance packages paid to CEOs since 2000. In total, the twenty-one CEOs included in the report had received severance pay of almost $4 billion in "walk-away" packages—each in excess of $100 million.

■ Gender Diversity Report

The focus of this report is on women in governance positions. It examines two related issues in corporate governance: poor board diversity and long tenures of board directors. Specifically, this report analyzes the potential effect of replacing various percentages of long-tenured male directors with women.

■ Appropriate ESG Behavior Reports

These reports are based upon how well a company is meeting its ESG obligations. It is, however, important to keep in mind that they are not all based on the same criteria and are also subject to the accuracy of the information provided them by a firm. Therefore, providers of ESG research and ratings still bear the burden of demonstrating the value of their data for mainstream investment managers, asset owners, and insurers.

In its report Behavioral ESG: Focusing on What Matters, GMI summarizes the evolving role of ESG metrics:

> [T]he new model is intended to highlight companies where significant gaps between compliance and behavior not only exist but are also most likely to impact investment returns. Where the original model was developed before Enron and Sarbanes-Oxley, the new model was developed after Dodd-Frank, BP Deepwater and the very significant corporate failures of the sub-prime crisis. The shift of focus from compliance-driven evenly weighted metrics to material context-weighted metrics has significantly increased the value of GMI Ratings' model to mainstream investors and insurers. In particular, the new model helps these decision-makers by assigning due weight to governance and executive compensation risks that undeniably affect corporate valuations.

One example of how GMI Ratings protect the interests of shareholders—and by extension, customers and clients—is through its Governance Insight Alert report. Published periodically, this report highlights firms that are in potential violation of the principles GMI Ratings seeks to uphold. While the report represents corporate negatives in its "Governance Spotlight" section, it also cites difficulties in the way companies handle environmental, social, accounting, and high risk misbehavior.

The following is an excerpt from one of these reports. It shows GMI's focus on a specific aspect of corporate bylaws in an effort to expand the shareholder's ability to file lawsuits against the corporations in which they have invested:

A few months ago, we noted the trend for companies to amend their bylaws to include "exclusive forum" provisions, which constrain shareholder lawsuits to the company's choice of venue. These bylaws weaken the ability of shareholders to use litigation as a monitoring tool on companies—and their unilateral imposition by boards raises other governance concerns.

Delaware courts recently gave another, potentially far more powerful tool to companies to shield themselves from shareholder derivative litigation: in May, the court gave the nod to "loser pays" bylaws, in which shareholder plaintiffs must pay the company's legal expenses if they fail to win the case. We've seen a few cases of these loser-pay bylaws in the Russell 3000: one at medical supplies manufacturer Biolase (BIOL), which implemented a narrowly targeted loser-pays bylaw, focused on the former CEO who has sued the company. At Lannett Company (LCI), however, the bylaw applies to all litigation. Not all shareholder litigation has merit, to be sure—but these unilaterally imposed bylaws provide boards with thick insulation from accountability to shareholders.

In addition to noting the legal challenges to a shareholder's influence over corporate operations in this report, GMI Ratings also cites governance red flags, such as the "threat of delisting," compromised "board independence," and a split between the Board Chairman and the CEO of one of the companies reviewed. In every case, the report gave the cited companies a grade of "C."

The report also cited three energy-related environmental concerns that caused GMI to give the offending companies "C" and "D" grades. Also cited were violations of "consumer safety" by a fast-food chain, a charge of "processing drug trafficking transactions" to a major bank, and the accusation of a technology company for "supply-chain child labor" violations. To these companies, GMI handed out grades ranging from "C" to "F."

To me, such oversight of corporate activity exemplifies the height of social responsibility. It also brings to light that the three general categories measuring a company's "responsibility quotient"—the environmental, social, and governance—are, in fact, inseparable from each other. Nowhere is this better demonstrated than in a letter written by Ceres president Mindy Lubber regarding the 2010 BP Gulf of Mexico oil spill. In it, she emphasizes how important it is "for all companies involved in deepwater drilling to be open and transparent with investors and stakeholders at this crucial historic moment." She wrote:

> [t]he shareholder harm that has flowed from the BP spill has focused investor attention on governance, compliance and management systems needed to minimize risks associated with deepwater offshore oil and gas development worldwide. The BP Gulf of Mexico disaster has also raised concerns about response plans by companies and the industry for dealing with offshore accidents.

In addition to demonstrating Ceres' focus on environmental issues, the letter strongly suggests that the three areas representing the concerns of social response investors are, in fact indivisible. It states how environmental concerns invariably overflow to include issues of governance and corporate responsibility, as well as social issues. These concerns also include corporate practices that prove contrary to the interests of those people affected.

THE SHIFTING CORPORATE SANDS
AND EMERGENCE OF NEW COMPANY POSITIONS

One of the key areas in which the adoption of ESG metrics has been most influential is in the executive function of the contemporary corporation. Where company executives and directors were once isolated from those with lesser positions in the management chain, today, those roles have changed dramatically.

I describe these new roles as "osmotic."

What were once corporate mansions surrounded by virtually impenetrable walls are now being transformed into organizations that are more osmotic, more transparent and accessible. No longer are corporate officers holed up in their brick-walled hideaways. They are now open to absorbing, processing, and presenting information to the public more clearly than ever before. Thanks to ESG metrics assuming an ever-more-important role, consumers are now able to put their fingers on the pulse of corporations more directly and accurately than ever before. Such awareness of a company's social responsiveness enables the public to rank them accordingly.

Where "good governance" once meant executive isolation, the term is now much more dependent on outside influence. Where earlier boards of directors were often slow to react to what are now recognized as social- and governance-related phenomena, the new global marketplace demands their immediate attention to issues that might have been swept under the corporate rug in the past. Now words such as "wisdom," "caution," and "reserve" have given way to the need for direct action, clarity of purpose, and sense of community. In other words, directors and executives are now paid to be aware of social demands and to react swiftly. If they don't, the severity of inaction often generates negative results.

The Chief Technology Officer

With the burgeoning technological environment that has emerged since the mid 1990s, successful new world companies have been compelled to add a Chief Technology Officer (CTO) to its list of executive positions. The primary duty of the CTO is overseeing the company's technological issues. It is a critical position, as corporations need to manage the new transparent and interconnected environment created by today's technology.

The Chief Relationship Officer

Another important change in corporate governance is the emergence of what I describe as the Chief Relationship Officer. Different companies have different names for this position—Chief Sustainability Officer, VP of External Affairs, VP of Government Relations—but its function is the same. Basically, this officer keeps an eye on the social needs and issues of the outside world and keeps the corporate leaders apprised of these public concerns. Basically, the person in this position strives to maintain good relationships between the company and the public.

Chief Relationship Officers don't "control" functions in the way, for example, that a Chief Corporate Counsel controls a firm's legal function or how CEOs control executive decisions. Instead, they make companies aware of what society is expecting of them. Boards of directors rely on them for this knowledge.

I have often worked with these relationship officers, who translate to their corporate officers what the world expects. They are the ones who identify the critical partners and associates that can advance the company's success. Their roles are becoming increasingly important in a world of "swift" communications whose consequences, if left unaddressed, can be very "severe." Society and social considerations need to be addressed by every corporation; the degree of success they have in listening and responding to what society is demanding of them is one of the keys to long-term success.

SUNCOR
CHAMPION OF SOCIAL AND GOVERNANCE PRACTICES

In the previous chapter, you saw how, through its practices, Suncor improved its corporate profile as a champion of the environment. Its concerns, however, did not end with the environment. As Suncor grew to become one of the largest energy companies in the world, with operations in over 100 countries, it created its own Social Responsibility Management System, which includes the Suncor Energy Foundation. This group, which includes proportional representation of First Nations from Canada's Wood Buffalo Region, serves as an example of a diversified workplace. Mel Benson, a member of Suncor's Board of Directors, is also a member of Alberta's Beaver Lake Cree Nation and winner of Canada's 2003 National Aboriginal Achievement Award. Benson hopes his presence on the board since 2000 "shortens the journey to equality" for indigenous peoples.

By working with indigenous peoples to make sure that they, too, benefit from the economic development that flows from oil exploration and extraction, they have stabilized access to their near future. Suncor has made several efforts to reach out to non-traditional stakeholders to help the company develop a plan to move closer to the goal of sustainability.

"Suncor's stakeholders are the compass that keeps us moving in the right direction—toward our vision of becoming a sustainable energy company," proclaimed Rick George, then-President and CEO of Suncor. Suncor was among the first oil companies in the world to start talking about sustainability. It has adopted a Standards of Business Conduct that includes a twenty-four-hour "Integrity Hotline," which gives employees a confidential venue for airing concerns about workplace problems and management practices.

An extensive 2006 review of the Suncor's corporate governance practices ensured that its board of operations is in compliance with the new guidelines that had been issued by the Toronto Stock Exchange, the New York Stock Exchange, and the Sarbanes-Oxley Act of the U.S. With workplace safety a top priority, Suncor launched its Journey to Zero program in 2002. This series of workshops and training programs is designed to reinforce employee awareness and accountability for safety in the workplace. In recognition of the success of the Journey to Zero initiative, Suncor was awarded the President's Canadian Operational Excellence Award in 2003.

CATERPILLAR
KEEPING THE SOCIAL METRIC IN FOCUS

Caterpillar is the world's largest manufacturer of construction and mining equipment, diesel and natural gas engines, industrial turbines, and diesel-electric locomotives in the world. In 2013 the company generated more than $31 billion in revenues worldwide. CAT, as it is commonly known, has established itself worldwide as a "genuine enabler of sustainable world progress and opportunity." The word "sustainable" characterizes one of the company's key focuses.

One thing that characterizes the Caterpillar "sustainability" campaign is that as an industrial manufacturing giant, much of its attention is directed toward the social component of ESG metrics. An example of how the company has become an ESG-conscious new world corporation is through the annual publication of its sustainability report since 2005. The 2014 report titled Local Citizen: Making Sustainable Progress Possible One Community at a

Time marked CAT as a company that always keeps the social metric in its sights. According to Caterpillar Chairman and CEO Douglas Oberhelman:

> [O]ur employees live in the communities near the Caterpillar facilities where they work, so we are personally interested in preserving and improving those communities. I think our people *are* proud of Caterpillar's work in their neighborhoods, all over the world. We've included just a few examples in this report, including employees in Nashville, Tenn., who provide pro bono legal services, and employees in Brazil, who are preserving native plants.
>
> The Caterpillar Foundation supports dozens and dozens of efforts like these through grants that are targeted to alleviate the root causes of poverty and provide paths to self-sufficiency and prosperity. Since its formation in 1952, the Caterpillar Foundation has given hundreds of millions of dollars to support sustainable progress for families and communities across the globe.

The company's commitment to the social metric appears on its website: We take seriously our responsibility to give back to the communities in which we work and live. The Caterpillar Foundation, founded in 1952, is helping to make sustainable progress possible around the world through support of environmental sustainability, access to education and fulfillment of basic human needs.

Among the many ways that Caterpillar sets itself apart as an environmentally conscious company is through the establishment of its Cat Reman remanufacturing program. As Caterpillar products reach the end of their productive lives, they are remanufactured and returned to like-new condition. Once restored, the products are sold in "same-as-new quality" with enormous savings to their purchasers. Material that cannot be used in the remanufacturing process is converted into reusable production-ready material. The Cat Reman program effectively doubles the lifespan of Caterpillar products.

Caterpillar is emerging this century as a new world company. While it continues to champion environmental sustainability through the development of efficient engines and machines, as well as advanced farm-related software, it has never lost sight of the fact that in the end, it is the people who matter.

SOCIAL RESPONSE CAPITALISM
FROM BUYER BEWARE TO BUYER BE HEARD

Since the banking crisis of 2008, corporate board members can no longer simply be a group of "high-powered friends." At the very least, they must possess basic financial literacy, while the

---

Flex
Social and Governance Support

Among the ways Flex supports ESG metrics is through its Corporate Social and Environmental (CSER) program. Included among this program's focus are People, Ethics, Governance, and Community Partnership. The purpose of their involvement in these three areas is to "continually improve our corporate citizenship and workplace performance." As a founding member and active participant in the Electronic Industry Citizenship Coalition (EICC), Flex demonstrates its commitment to these values. The EICC code of conduct specifies "that working conditions in the electronics industry supply chain are safe, that workers are treated with respect and dignity, and that business operations are environmentally responsible and conducted ethically."

heads of key committees must have viable financial training and operational experience.

In many European companies, board members can no longer be all male. Germany, for instance, recently passed a law requiring that at least 30 percent of the directorial positions of many large European companies be filled by women. Norway, Spain, France, and Iceland had already set the gender minimum for directorial positions at 40 percent, while in Belgium and the Netherlands, that number is 30 percent. It seems very likely that this important social metric will be coming to the United States soon.

Social and governance principles are increasingly becoming an integral part of corporate policies and practices. They are making companies more inclusive and more responsive to the interests of clients and customers, and of those who are instrumental in setting governance policies and standards.

CONCLUSION

While the social metric can be applied to many innovative and far-reaching company practices, there is clear evidence that it works. Incorporating social elements makes a firm last longer, perform more productively, and get better rankings in terms of loyalty and workplace satisfaction.

In today's world, where ESG reigns and the leadership intangibles often matter more than physical assets, these new world values are a reflection of society itself. Globally, society is rapidly becoming more diverse and more creative than ever before. We have long passed the time when successful firms are run largely by the "engineering class." Now there is so much creativity in the area of product design, so many sophisticated and inspired marketing teams, and so much promise emerging for the near future. It is no longer about the quantity of goods created or services provided.

Today, with social and governance metrics being acknowledged as important indicators of long-term success, shared leadership is rapidly becoming what matters most. Social response capitalism is in no small part, measured by how fast and how effectively a firm can respond to public expectations. The corporate mansion now sits in a public neighborhood. More and more, people are free to peer through the windows and access the premises.

Further, the people now given company access are not just *Wall Street Journal* reporters, but anyone with access to the Internet. Company information from carbon disclosure reports to Dow Jones Sustainability Asset Management Reports are available around the globe. This data accessibility enables anyone—not simply stockholders—to exert pressure on corporations in the way they are run. In a sense, the lens through which we can peer into the corporate mansion has caused the gradual disappearance of the mansion itself, transforming it into a structure that is much more accessible.

Questions can now be asked directly to corporations, often through social media. Leadership teams at every level must maintain an awareness of events outside their companies and respond accordingly. The new "world on our wrist" has enabled this merger of metrics.

When corporations attend responsibly to the social and governance metrics that affect their businesses directly, they invariably find that people are more likely to make purchase decisions based on those criteria. What we are seeing is the expansion of corporate stakeholders to include governments at all levels, social advocacy groups, and analyzers of investment and business trends. When we say social response capitalism, we mean a twenty-first century form of capitalism in which firms compete not only on price and quality, but also on social and governance issues.

4

Money Matters

Lessons from the Past

Remember Compaq, E.F. Hutton, American Motors, MCI WorldCom, Pan American Airways, Woolworth's, and Eastern Airlines? Each of these corporate giants was a household name, yet by the year 2000 they were all out of business. And they represent just a handful of failed major businesses. Even more disturbing, of the Fortune 500 corporations, it is estimated that nearly 60 percent have performed poorly over the past four decades.

What is going on? In an effort to answer that question, I'd like to start by focusing on the 2008 failure of Lehman Brothers investment firm. What started out in the mid-1800s as a small commodities-trading operation founded by three frugal immigrant brothers grew to become one of the largest, most successful financial services firms in the world. Its failure came as the result of widespread greed within the financial industry that had grown to unmanageable proportions . . . and the fact that although the Federal government had bailed out other equally greedy banks and financial giants, it refused to bail out Lehman Brothers.

The demise of Lehman Brothers represented the end result of unreliable economic policies that began in the early 1970s. The company went under as the result of an economy that had reached a tipping point in 2008. While there were a number of causes of the 2008 economic crash, they can all be summed up in two critical terms: speculative capitalism and excessive financialization. With *speculative capitalism*, focus has shifted away from the responsible provision of goods and services to the creation of questionable assets—assets that have no connection to the real world we live in, but have, nonetheless, taken on a life of their own. Due to the shift away from measuring goods and services, determining the value of financial assets depends almost exclusively on financial manipulation. This *financialization* involves the investing of a company's liquid assets into equities strictly on the basis of getting the greatest short-term return—with little or no attention paid to the stability of the equity.

Management guru Peter Drucker has spoken powerfully about how money and the issues it creates are seldom managed well from within. He has emphasized that the way firms manage money—or more often than not, mismanage it—explains why the true value of a firm often remains hidden, or is distorted, or gets squandered. The dramatic global economic downturn that began in 2008 and the revelation of widespread irresponsible corporate behavior— poor transparency and inadequate risk management—that largely contributed to it, only reinforced Drucker's lasting set of messages.

Drucker's analysis is certainly on point. However, in order to better understand what has happened to our current economy, we need to examine in greater detail the economic forces that have been at play over the past forty-plus years. This chapter takes a fresh look at how responsible capitalism has been gradually corrupted by greed, self-interest, and unchecked financial manipulation.

FOR THE LOVE OF MONEY

By 2008, the U.S. economy had for nearly four decades been gradually shifting. It went from an economy built and sustained on the steady growth of businesses that were based on commodities, goods, and services to one that relied on the unchecked growth of speculative capitalism.

This excess began in 1971, when the country's government debt was growing more rapidly than the economy could support. Many of the nations holding U.S. debts began demanding settlements, not with dollars but with gold. In response, then-President Richard Nixon, rather than endanger the nation's gold supply, decided to take the U.S. dollar off the gold standard. By eliminating this connection, he began the financialization or manipulation of the economy. At the same time, he unleashed the floodgates of speculative capitalism.

It was a time when the famous Latin phrase *radix malorum est cupiditas* was used to describe how the financial industry conducted business. Often incorrectly translated as "money is the root of evil," these words actually say "the *love of money* is the root of all evil." This is an important distinction to keep in mind when considering the role of money with regard to corporate success or failure.

People *do* love the things money can buy. The problems surface when they take that love of money to a point where it becomes an obsession (as many analysts and brokers have done). There is nothing wrong with loving the things money can buy. That's why companies are able to sell us cars and homes, and encourage us to make purchases that will help us better enjoy our lives. Of course, it's no secret that advertisers lure consumers with promises that their products will provide everything from improved lifestyles to radiant beauty and true love. But as a savvy consumer, you know not to believe everything a commercial may promise. In the same way, you cannot believe speculative capitalists, who base their analyses and recommendations exclusively on the lust of money.

THE END OF THE GOLDEN DOLLAR

In the early 1970s, economist Milton Friedman was boldly asserting that money was the only thing that mattered when measuring corporate success or failure with quotes such as: "[T]he social responsibility of business is to increase its profits." At the same time, many of the nations that held our debt were knocking at our door as they tried to exchange their dollars for gold. In response, then-President Richard Nixon announced that the value of the U.S. dollar would no longer be tied to the fixed price of gold, which was valued then at $35.00 per ounce. This may have been a clever political decision, but it was ripe with a few unintended consequences.

Rather than let them clean out Fort Knox, Nixon took the dollar off the gold standard. In doing so, he introduced a world in which the value of currencies—no longer tied to a fixed-price commodity such as gold—began to be determined by globally trading them in pairs against each other on the Foreign Exchange (Forex) market. This ushered in the age of *fiat currency*, currency printed by the government whose value is not pegged to gold. At the same time, the value of the U.S. dollar declined dramatically in relation to gold for numerous reasons.

At the same time the value of U.S. currency was plummeting, the country's economic growth declined from an annual average of 4 percent in the years following World War II to 2.9 percent since the mid-1980s. By the 1990s, with the dollar's value rapidly falling to the point where it was worth less than 10 percent of the rising price of gold, the Forex market began a period of rapid global growth. Today, the Forex is the largest market in the world. According to the Bank for International Settlements (BIS), by early 2012, the volume of the currencies traded had reached more than $5 trillion daily. To put that into perspective, the Forex market trades more money each day than the U.S. National debt owes.

Over time, the consequences of Nixon's decision were socially profound. It is estimated that the average annual income of Americans is now 50 percent less than it would have been if the dollar had remained on the gold standard. The country has gone from a modest national trade surplus in 1971 to a trade deficit that is now greater than $400 billion annually. The combined federal, state, and local tax base is now some 50 percent smaller than it would have been had we remained on the gold standard. Indeed, these changes helped usher in global capitalization.

In other words, the average American has been impacted by this change from a gold-based currency to one that is at the mercy of a small band of elite speculative capitalists. The more the economy is dependent on the actions of this group, rather than on the hard work, entrepreneurship, and savings of everyday Americans, the poorer the country becomes.

With the rise of speculative capitalism, financial corruption had spread throughout the world by 2008. This battle is classic, recurrent, and consequential.

Letting in the Bulls

The devaluation of U.S. currency was exacerbated by several other factors, including the repeal of the 1933 Glass-Steagall Act. Based on the belief that speculative bank activities were instrumental in causing the Stock Market Crash of 1929, which lead to the Great Depression, the Glass-Steagall Act was passed. This act made it illegal for banks to serve as investment brokers, effectively limiting their services. No longer could banks invest money from customer accounts, nor could they loan money to clients based on credit-worthiness.

With the repeal of Glass-Steagall in 1999, the major banks, which had lobbied hard for the change, were able to take the money in their customers' savings and checking accounts and "invest" it in the now global equity markets. In addition, new government requirements made it easier for people with sub-prime credit to obtain mortgages. The result was a deluge of high-debt mortgages that were granted to unqualified borrowers. The mortgages were underwritten by the government agencies Fannie Mae and Freddie Mac and financed by bankers. The repeal of Glass-Steagall also enabled banks to become investment brokers by creating and marketing their own sub-prime mortgage-backed securities. This contributed significantly to the bubble that finally burst in 2008.

The Fed Steps In

If it had ended there—if Glass-Steagall had been reinstated and the sub-prime mortgage-backed securities issued by banks had wound down with adequate supervision—we might have been able to navigate our way out of the financial woods. In reality, though, the Federal Reserve Bank (Fed) made matters worse by instituting the practice of *quantitative easing* (QE). In a legitimate attempt to stimulate the economy, this unconventional monetary policy enabled the Fed to print about $4 trillion (what some see as the equivalent of counterfeit money) and then use that money to buy back a small portion of the toxic derivatives created and held by the largest banks.

Although the big banks had hundreds of billions of dollars worth of QE money at their disposal, they did not, as in the past, lend it to regional corporations, which would have created jobs and improved the economy in America. Instead, in the years following the 2008 crash, banks funneled most of the money they received from the Fed into the global stock market. This helped create a huge run-up of stock prices, inflating the value of equities far beyond what the performance of most companies warranted— a prime example of speculative capitalism.

Another Fed policy that has been a key factor in devaluating the savings of Americans is its Zero Interest Rate Policy (ZIRP). By maintaining interest rates at or near zero, ZIRP was designed to hold down the amount of money owed on the country's dramatically increasing national debt. This policy has cost the American people upwards of $1 trillion due to the fact that they receive almost no interest on money they keep in savings accounts. This is another consequence of allowing speculative capitalism to proceed with blind enthusiasm.

Market Mayhem

Some Americans have also been driven out of the stock market by the dramatic increase in computer-generated stock trades. Nearly three quarters of all stock trades are now made by what can only be described as robot-computers. These computer-generated trades frequently involve hundreds of thousands of shares of stock, and they are carried out in milliseconds. They create huge profits for those few managing them, even though each trade moves a stock's value by only fractional amounts. And though stock prices have been driven to record heights, the number of Americans who actually own stocks has dropped dramatically. In 2007, before the crash, 65 percent of Americans owned stocks. By 2013, that number had dropped to 52 percent.

There's an even more dramatic statistic to demonstrate how speculative capitalists have commandeered the global economy through financial manipulation and have shut out the average American from participation. Since the 2008 crash, the top 10 percent of the wealthiest people in the country have received *118 percent* of the income growth generated in what has been at best a tepid recovery! The bottom 90 percent of Americans actually saw their real income drop by 18 percent between 2009 and 2012. New world companies know this is not sustainable for long.

When a government, along with a speculative capitalist economic culture, creates such an imbalance between average Americans and the financial elite, it distorts the relationship between these two groups to the point at which they essentially become enemies—opposing tribes in all deeds and social attitudes. What has emerged is an increasingly vicious and severe battle between speculative capitalism and social response capitalism. In this battle, it is the lives of the people that are at stake, and they are being compromised by the forces of speculative capitalism.

There has been and continues to be an inordinate amount of pressure by speculative capitalists to shrink rules and grow money. This has led to economic distortions that have downplayed and minimized the power of science and innovation. It has enabled the global economic elite to "financialize" the economy in such a way that fewer innovation dollars go into businesses that create and expand legitimate products, goods, and services. Instead, all of the money created goes to a new class of investors who are not playing by the ESG and social rules. Instead, they are cashing in at the expense of small and mid-size individual investors and the brokers who represent them. The "investor elite" choose stocks whose values have been exponentially over-inflated.

CAN SOCIAL RESPONSE CAPITALISM REVERSE OUR ECONOMIC DECLINE?

What occurred from the early 1970s to 2008 is eye-opening social history—and something not taught in American History classes. Although the forces of speculative capitalism have had a profoundly negative effect on the world of business, the news is not all bad. During that time, social response capitalism—a force for good— has emerged. And it has provided a foundation on which to minimize and ultimately eliminate the negative effects of speculative capitalism. It encourages a new way of doing business that is based on environmental, social, and governance principles.

For corporations, social response capitalism means a move away from the position that only money matters to one that encourages a responsible operation that not only maintains profitability, but also increases and sustains it. It also means that people have the opportunity to reclaim their rights as consumers and investors. Today, enabled by a more transparent and immediately accessible world, we have an unprecedented opportunity to patronize and invest in companies that earn our loyalty, rather than give in to the forces that are trying to take us in exactly the opposite direction.

Social response capitalism offers more than a glimmer of hope. While the economy is a strong influence on whether corporations succeed or fail, we have learned that there are more important indicators that determine the likelihood of corporate success. The fact that we have endured significant economic decline in the past forty years has been a strong influence on the way new world companies now define corporate responsiveness and good corporate governance. As we move away from what was once a single-focus vision on money as the measure of economic success, we are moving closer to a more responsive and agile way of looking at money's influence on how businesses can best thrive and adapt to social needs.

ESG METRICS

The quality, price, and performance of a company's products and services have always had a major impact on a firm's stock value. But today, issues that were once invisible or ignored can help us to better determine a company's true value. These issues are the ESG metrics.

As explained in the earlier chapters, in the broadest sense, ESG metrics represent issues associated with environmental, social, and corporate governance policies and practices. These categories have for a long time been seen as "intangibles" —not easily measured. Using them to determine a company's worth has been like using such words as "heart" and "competitiveness" to determine the worth of an athlete. Everyone is aware that they are important characteristics, but until fairly recently, no one has understood how to measure their value.

We are now, in fact, making significant progress in determining how to quantify once-hidden "intangibles" such as superior management. We can now more accurately calculate how well companies are serving the interests of society at large, and link that to the likelihood that they will remain profitable in the long run. We have discovered that: *Assessing a company's value on the basis of ESG metrics actually provides a better measure of its worth and its prospects for future success than focusing exclusively on its short-term balance sheet.* ESG metrics are not simply the keys to sustainability with regard to environmental, social, and governance measures, but to financial sustainability as well. They provide a critical lens through which we can better calibrate the value and success of our investments. We use these metrics to predict financial success in many ways, including the following:

- Analyzing ESG risks across asset classes and integrating the results into the evaluation of our portfolios.

- Understanding the physical risks to infrastructure, real estate, and supply chains based on forecast environmental impacts.

- Preparing for new regulatory frameworks that may impact traditional industries and energize new emerging industries.

One key question we must ask is: "How accurate are the predictions and valuations of corporate worth when they are based on ESG metrics?" There are several components to consider in answering this critical question. First, conventional measures of corporate worth still matter. But profit and loss are no longer the only drivers of corporate success. As social response capitalism continues to gain recognition, and as the importance of ESG metrics in determining company worth becomes better understood, corporate success is becoming increasingly dependent on reliable ESG measurements.

A revolution based on ESG metrics is changing the world of corporate valuation. The view of these measures seen as "intangibles" is now changing. As third-party rating groups grow in their influence, it is now being demonstrated, industry by industry and company by company, that it is not simply possible but critically important to attach a "risk premium" based on ESG metrics to the value of stocks in every sector.

To this ESG list, I would like to add another important "S" component: *sustainability*. When a corporation scores high in ESG values, the financial sustainability of the enterprise itself improves, along with its movement toward promoting and protecting the sustainability of the resources it uses.

Over the past fifteen years, new measures of these metrics have developed and become increasingly sophisticated. They have grown to include thousands of corporations worldwide. They measure and examine values that had previously been ignored, even as the global economy was evolving from its exclusive dependence on the "profit metric" to a place where the inclusion of environmental, social, and governance metrics became important components in evaluating corporate prospects for success. In the process, they have also expanded to include information on the way companies are perceived by the public, itemizing the true costs of reputation as well as operational risks to the value of a firm.

INDEXING A COMPANY'S INTANGIBLE VALUE

Our advance into the new century marked a turning point. In 2000, Cap Gemini Ernst & Young's Center for Business Innovation articulated its own recommendations for measuring corporate intangibles in an article titled "The value creation index: quantifying intangible value." As the article explains, Cap Gemini developed its Value Creation Index (VCI) because "[t]oday's economy—one based on assets like knowledge, R&D and innovation—requires an unprecedented challenge: valuing intangible assets." The piece went on to explain why such metrics have become so important: "Corporate investments in brand development, leadership training, and R&D now exceed total investments in tangible assets."

Simply stated, these ESG metrics have assumed dramatically increasing importance as measures of corporate prospects for success. Furthermore, the authors asserted that at least a third of a mature company's value is attributable to non-financial information; for smaller cap companies, the proportion is even larger.

The Cap Gemini article followed immediately in the wake of another important business intangibles milestone: the creation of The Dow Jones Sustainability Index (DJSI) in 1999. This index was created for the purpose of monitoring the performance of companies in areas that had not been included in previous assessments of their financial worth. It is based on information obtained through the RobecoSAM Corporate Sustainability Assessment (CSA). Each year, over 3,000 publicly traded companies across fifty-nine different industries are invited to participate. Of these, the largest 2,500 global companies by market capitalization are eligible for inclusion in the flagship DJSI world.

The CSA questionnaires contain from 80 to 120 questions designed to measure the sustainability of the participating corporations. In addition to general questions that are asked across industries, at least half of each questionnaire deals with "industry-specific risks and opportunities that focus on economic, environmental, and social challenges and trends" that exert a strong influence on the company's prospects for future success. Those industries are identified in Standard & Poor's Global Industry Classification Standard (GICS).

The CSA also focuses on the "media coverage and other publicly available information" regarding such issues as "labor disputes, accidents, [and] human rights abuses," social and gover-nance metrics that are now seen, not simply as relevant, but very important to a company's prospects. The fact that the survey is broken down by industry "reflects RobecoSAM's conviction that industry-specific sustainability opportunities and risks play a key role in a company's long-term success, and allow RobecoSAM to compare companies against their own peers in order to identify sustainability leaders."

This increasing focus on the value of intangibles as predictors of a company's success and sustainability resulted in greater demand for global transparency. Equity investors were able to know more and with greater accuracy about the actual risks and potential rewards of their investments. As you will see in the next chapter, the more analysts relied upon non-financial performance factors, the more accurate their earnings forecasts became.

CHAMPIONS OF
SOCIAL RESPONSE CAPITALISM

In the years following the crash of 2008, the cause of responsible investing has been advanced significantly by key players in two organizations: Morgan Stanley Capital International (MSCI) and Bloomberg L.P. Two ESG champions—Hewson Baltzell, the Executive Director of MSCI, and Lenora Suki, Senior Strategist and Sustainability Product Lead for Bloomberg—and the organi-zations in which they play leading roles have worked diligently and with great success to bring ESG metrics data into the mainstream of strategic investment risk analysis. MSCI does the heavy lifting of capturing the data necessary to enable investors to assess the sustainability practices of the companies they invest in; Bloomberg digests the data and gets it out to investors in such a way that they can take it into account. No pun intended.

Hewson Baltzell has been a leader in the emergence of ESG investing for over twenty years. In 1998, he became the co-founder and president of Innovest, the first company to focus on ESG investment. I use the term "first" advisedly: Baltzell and his firm originated the practice of rating companies according to environmental, social, and governance performances.

Created by Baltzell and his team for Innovest, Figure 4.1 below uses the image of an iceberg to signify a company's financial measures. The iceberg's very small visible tip represents the conventional set of *tangible* criteria used to measure a firm's financial worth. Measurable in terms of standard accounting, these criteria do not fully represent of the true social and commercial drivers of a firm. That aspect is represented by the hidden portion of the iceberg, which contains four non-financial *intangible* "value drivers." According to Innovest, these drivers—stakeholder capital,

Figure 4.1. The Iceberg Balance Sheet

Innovest uses the concept of an iceberg to represent the criteria used in determining a company's financial worth. The very small tip of the iceberg represents financial capital—the conventional, *tangible* criteria used—while the larger hidden portion represents four *intangible* value drivers. These hidden aspects take into account such factors as human talent, innovation, and alliance building.

human capital, eco values, and sustainable governance—take into account such factors as human talent, innovation, and alliance building. They are the hidden elements that are key in assessing the worth of a new world company. In its totality, this "iceberg of value" is more accurate and more reliable in determining a company's worth than financial diagnostics alone.

In 2009, Innovest was purchased by RiskMetrics Group, and Baltzell became Head of Product Development, Environmental, Social & Governance Research. Little more than a year later, Risk-Metrics was purchased by MSCI, and Baltzell became Head of Product Development—ESG Research. By 2015, Baltzell headed a team of some 230 people in offices around the world, and it has become the leading force in the promotion of ESG investment.

MSCI now evaluates the ESG performance of more than 6,000 companies in nearly 100 industries. Baltzell's team manages ESG investments for over 600 clients and has more than $2.3 trillion under management. MSCI also participates in a joint venture with Barclays that provides ESG metrics for fixed income products, including the sovereign bonds of individual countries. In Baltzell's words, "We provide the tools asset owners and global asset managers use to measure and manage ESG risk and opportunity . . . [and] we have been able to achieve many of our goals that had been unattainable when we were independent." Having reached this peak, Hewson left MSCI in late 2015 to join a new powerhouse, Just Capital. Yet the mainstreaming of ESG into MSCI remains powerfully intact, and massively consequential. The history of Just Capital is yet to be written over the next decades.

Another key player in the field is Bloomberg's Lenora Suki. She has been instrumental in converting the voluminous and complex ESG data generated by MSCI into an easily accessible format that resembles a dashboard. Available at Bloomberg terminals, this data is able to be utilized for making investment decisions. It is an important tool in the further mainstreaming of ESG metrics for a broad community of investors.

Among the other key analytic tools Bloomberg has introduced is its "Carbon Risk Valuation Tool." This tool was developed in response to the fear that climate change might "lead governments to mandate energy companies to keep a significant portion of their oil, gas and coal reserves 'stranded' in the ground." This tool helps protect the millions of Bloomberg clients against losses that might occur if these policies are implemented.

With this data, Bloomberg has been able to develop a range of sustainability products, including ESG rating tools and carbon risk tools that enable investors to integrate real-time ESG data into their investment analyses. Information based on investor analyses conducted by Bloomberg tells us that sustainability products are experiencing double-digit growth with regard to the number of unique users and volume of data utilized in making investment decisions. In addition to its energy/environmental data, Bloomberg incorporates governance data for over 11,000 companies and executive compensation for 16,000 companies. This is the new testament for new world companies. It forms their playbook for measuring performance.

QUANTIFYING INTANGIBLE VALUE DRIVERS

With the introduction of its Value Creation Index in 2000, Cap Gemini attempted to quantify the correlation between so-called "social value drivers" and stock performance. The introduction of this new metric provided an important summary of how these measures could be quantified in a systematic way. The VCI weighs each value driver category (e.g., alliances, brand, and innovation) according to its impact on a stock's value. Many common perceptions regarding what drives a company's value were redefined by the VCI. This took the thoughts of economists Peter Drucker and E.F. Schumacher and made them real and operational in the world of investments.

For example, while most twentieth-century executives expect items such as technology and customer satisfaction to be very important in determining a firm's future stock value, the VCI has demonstrated that they are somewhat less consequential than formerly assumed. And though most business leaders still do not give much credence to the relative importance of alliances, the VCI showed that companies with a variety of partnerships have substantially higher value and growth rates than firms that try to go it alone. It is as if the ability to align with others, a measure of the "social" metric of a business, is a good surrogate measure for sound management and leadership. Where in the years before, the VCI hard assets alone had been the basis of investors' confidence in the value of a firm's stock, the twenty-first century VCI findings introduced an important variable. This variable demonstrated that companies relying upon strategic alliances had discovered a method to achieve economies of scale in a new, more socially responsive way.

THE ROAD AHEAD

Is all of this social "sustainable value" and "responsiveness" talk nothing more than shifting sand? The answer is complex. Certainly classical measures of hard assets still matter, but it is becoming clear that they matter much less than had once been assumed. We are beginning to realize that a bloodless revolution—one based on the value of a company's intangibles—is occurring, and it is changing the worlds of corporate management and investing. Third-party rating groups are demonstrating, industry by industry and company by company, that it is now possible to attach a "risk premium" that takes into account the "intangible" metrics onto the value of every company's stock.

Despite the enormous advances in developing ESG metrics and demonstrating their effectiveness as predictors of success, there are still doubters. As analyst Joel Makower puts it, "sustainability leaders don't impress Wall Street." In his article of the same title, Makower asks, "If sustainable business practices create profits and shareholder value, why aren't mainstream investors paying attention?" He points out that, although a number of investment management firms are focusing strongly on the importance of intangibles as a measure of a business's prospects for success, he doubts that they are in control of enough investment dollars to move markets. The overriding reason for the lack of investor interest in sustainability is what the author, paraphrasing actor Strother Martin's memorable line in the film *Cool Hand Luke*, calls "a multi-million dollar failure to communicate."

In other words, until recently, corporate communicators haven't been able to get the data out to investors successfully, so they haven't been able to make the case regarding how sustainability creates "shareholder value." They have also had difficulty getting the message across to the public. However, as you will see in the next chapter, things are changing rapidly. Makower's negativite viewpoint forms an early warning. To gauge the true worth of these new metrics more accurately, we need to look to some leaders in the field to learn what their experience has shown.

ESG, SASB, and CDP and the Principle of Disclosure

At this point, I'd like to present some terms and acronyms that are critical to understanding how far the importance of ESG metrics has come. I will also be introducing some of the key champions of social response capitalism—leaders who are driving an ESG revo-

lution in investing that is rapidly gaining acceptance as a significant market mover.

Bruce Kahn is a man of two worlds. First, he holds a PhD in
Land Sciences from the University of Wisconsin; second, between
2005 and 2012, he was the Director and Senior Investment Analyst of Deutsche Bank's Climate Change Investment Research
Advisors. Deutsche Bank has consistently been rated at or near the
top of all financial organizations with regard to its sustainability
culture and policies. Its statement of purpose, which appears on its
website, explains its position this way:

> We want to create sustainable value: for our clients and
> employees, our shareholders and for society. Our goal is
> clear: Our high-performance culture must go hand-in-hand
> with a culture of responsibility.

Kahn now holds two important positions in the world of
finance. He manages a portfolio for Sustainable Investment Capital Management (SICM), and is on the advisory council for the
Sustainability Accounting Standards Board (SASB). His experience and the scientific rigor he brings to his work give him a
unique perspective on the emergence and growing influence of
ESG metrics.

Another organization, the Carbon Disclosure Project (CDP),
has played an important role in the arrival of ESG metrics as critical indicators of future corporate financial success. The organization sees its role as "driving sustainable economies":

> The CDP is an independent non-profit organization that
> holds the largest database of corporate climate change data in
> the world. Launched in the year 2000, 5,000 organizations
> from over 60 countries are now disclosing their greenhouse
> gas emissions and climate change strategies through the CDP.

In 2013, SICM, CDP, and financial advisory firm Pricewater-houseCoopers released an eye-opening report. Co-authored by Kahn, the report contains a startling revelation: The top-ranked 20 percent of the 702 companies monitored in the CDP's Global 500 climate change reports between 2008 and 2013 "provide a higher return on equity (+5.2 percent), more stable cash flow generation (+18.1 percent) and higher dividend growth (+1.6 percent)." In other words, the better a company's ESG metrics performance, the better the financial return to investors and the more financially stable the company.

Kahn also values the degree of ESG disclosure in which companies engage. He asserts that the degree of disclosure should lead to a "repricing of risk," because the greater a company's attention to ESG metrics and its transparency in these issues, the greater the likelihood it will improve its financial performance:

> If one associates a high CDP disclosure score with long term planning and risk management capability, it is possible that the stability of the defensive sectors makes them more conducive to, and rewarding of, what we typically think of as "good management practice." On the other hand, management teams in cyclical sectors may need to be more attuned to the short-term business risks and opportunities, and are more likely to be rewarded for optimizing performance over the cycle. We would therefore expect them to allocate resources to activities that maximize ROI in the short term, and less likely to focus on projects that take a long-term view, such as reporting to CDP.

Clearly then, when we focus our attention on longer-term investment goals rather than exclusively on quarterly profit-and-loss performance, we find that companies with strong ESG performances produce better returns than their non-ESG-compliant competitors.

Tracking ESG Performance

SASB releases its "Provisional Sustainability Accounting Standards" documents according to industry sectors. These publications outline "the minimum set of sustainability issues" for each of the seven industries monitored. Reports are available for Health Care, Financials, Technology & Communication, Non-Renewable Resources, Transportation, and Services, with additional reports released periodically. They are designed to be "decision useful for investors." SASB's development process for these documents is based on data provided by Bloomberg and includes a period in which public comments are received and integrated into the reports and a final review by an independent standards council.

In an interview my team led with Kahn in July of 2014, he predicted that "if SASB releases standards in 2016 and has full implementation by 2017, by 2020 a pricing correction due to reassessment of risk should happen." He went further in his assessment of how investors should regard this:

> There are people who talk about what the world should look like in the future as society deals with its major problems and there is what society will probably look like in the future. Smart investors invest in the overlap between what the world should look like and what it will likely look like.

ESG Influencers

Another influential player in the promotion of ESG metrics is Tim Smith, Senior Vice President of the Environmental, Social and Governance Group of Walden Asset Management. Prior to joining Walden in 2000, he had been with the Interfaith Center on

Corporate Responsibility (ICCR) as its executive director for nearly a quarter of a century. ICCR's mission is to bring social issues to the attention of corporations and to advise its clients in this area as they develop investment portfolios. Smith, who earned a bachelor's degree from the University of Toronto and a master's degree in Divinity from Union Theological Seminary, oversaw the growth of ICCR from 6 Protestant organizations to 275 religious institution investors.

Smith has been a member of numerous social responsibility-focused groups, including the Board of Social Investment Forum, of which he was the chairman of the board for five years; a South Africa development fund; World Neighbors; and the Kimberly-Clark Sustainability Advisory Board. He is also a member of the United Methodist Church Pension and Health Benefits Board. In 2007, Smith was named one of top 100 most influential people in Business Ethics by the Ethisphere Institute, which describes itself as "the global leader in defining and advancing the standards of ethical business practices that fuel corporate character, market-place trust and business success."

It was a passion for engagement on social issues that led Smith to Walden Asset Management. Walden had been engaged in responsible investing since the mid-1970s. At that time, it became involved in a divestment campaign focused on minimizing invest-ments in South African companies that supported apartheid. Smith's current position as chair of Walden's Environmental, Social and Governance Group enables him to engage with compa-nies regarding key ESG issues.

Smith describes the state of ESG investing this way: "We are currently going through a turning point with ESG. Compared to ten to twenty years ago, it's a whole new world, not just new dis-closure requirements and voluntary codes for investment, but companies are understanding and endorsing sustainability issues." He believes that it is "better to have a strong voice backed by

ownership [and] engage through proxy voting and other engagement plans to change company decision making."

In his own words, Smith understands that "combating climate
change is an uphill battle" and often "hard to integrate into business decisions." He maintains, however, that in the past decade,
much progress has been made in bringing awareness of ESG metrics to both corporations, whose principles and practices he works
at changing, and investors and investment managers. He feels
these groups are rapidly coming to realize that the analysis of ESG
metrics is one of the pillars of investment success.

Another important player in the progress of social response
capitalism is Mindy Lubber, the president of the Coalition for
Environmentally Responsible Economies (Ceres). Lubber was
introduced in Chapter 3 for her aggressive approach in holding
energy companies accountable for more responsive energy extraction practices.

All of these "players" have an important role in the advancement
of investor awareness regarding ESG metrics. As you have seen,
these new measures are also growing in importance, not only in
the decisions of investors, but also in the decisions and behavior of
corporate leaders. It is becoming increasingly clear that while "it is
money that matters" it takes much broader focus to ensure success.

CONCLUSION

In the 1987 movie *Wall Street*, Michael Douglas' character, Gordon
Gekko, takes the floor during a shareholders meeting. He calmly
and persuasively points out that "Greed is good." It is a virtue to
extol; a virtue to make money for the company's stockholders. During the years that followed *Wall Street*, our financial leaders seemed
to operate under that same exclusive philosophy. With the repeal of
the Glass-Steagall Act in 1999—which allowed the Gordon Gekkos

of the world to take over the banking institutions—the die was cast. We gradually abandoned the principles of true capitalism—a system based on free markets overseen by necessary but limited regulation—and turned reliable "corporate money" into what has become synonymous with "greed and corruption."

This chapter has shown how speculative capitalism, with help from a submissive national government, has enabled the largest banks to gain dominance in the world of finance and investing. It has also shown how social response capitalism and the companies that base their success on following its principles and practices represent the answer to a corporate world that has gone off track.

The key takeaway is this: The emergence of social response capitalism is on the rise. Through its growing influence, socially responsive businesses are returning their focus to the creation and delivery of meaningful goods and services. This is being done in such a way that the people of the world, not the financial elite, are the enduring winners in this ongoing struggle.

Social Response Investing

Protecting Your Portfolio

orporations are now among the most powerful and influential entities in the world. Consider the following: *Of the world's 100 largest financial entities in 2012, only 60 were countries. The other 40 were corporations.* Expanding that number from 100 to 150, corporations represented nearly 60 percent of the largest revenue-generators in the world. Without a doubt, the way in which these companies manage their operations has a profound effect on virtually all of the 7 billion souls with whom we share our planet. When these mega-corporations are truly socially responsive, our lives are made better in ways that governments cannot match, let alone compete with. As you will see, this is critically important not only to the investment community, but also to the future well-being of firms, your friends, and your family.

The previous chapter presented an overview of speculative capitalism and explained how it led to the financial collapse of 2008. The focus of this chapter is two-fold. First, it shows how the fallout resulting from speculative capitalism can be corrected through the adoption of the principles and practices of social response capitalism. Second, it offers helpful data-gathering guidelines for investing in socially responsive companies. You will discover how to identify the key marketing analysts and investment advisors who understand the importance of social response capitalism and who encourage the support of companies that follow ESG principles. By understanding how to measure the responsible business practices of new world companies, you can improve your investment portfolio's chances of long-term success.

ACCESSING THE MARKET

Let's start with an important historical trend regarding the ebb and flow in stock ownership over the past forty years. Historically, stock ownership was dominated by the rich and powerful. For the most part, this "elite" group was able to greatly influence the course of the market. Even the system in place for the buying and selling of shares seemed to favor the brokers, whose hefty fees discouraged the average person from investing.

In the 1960s, Charles Schwab launched a new type of brokerage company. By charging lower, less punitive fees, Schwab opened up the market to more middle-class investors. With the establishment of Individual Retirement Accounts (IRAs) in 1974 and 401(k) plans in 1978, Wall Street suddenly became the "people's market." Baby Boomers were able to use the growth of the market to invest in their retirement.

By the 1990s, more and more people—not only in America, but throughout the world—owned stock. Unfortunately, since the start of the new century, this trend has been moving backward. This is thanks, in large part, to the reassertion by speculative capitalists of an irresponsible, not to say an often "corrupt," approach to investing.

A great portion of the trillions of dollars in unsecured fiat currency printed by the Federal Reserve Bank since 2009 has found its way into the stock market. This caused the inflation of stock values far beyond what their real-world financial performance merited. What resulted was a greatly over-valued stock market that had effectively closed out many individual investors and smaller investment management companies.

At the same time, however, there has been an ongoing increase in the knowledge regarding investment principles based on social response capitalism. As that new force asserts itself, the markets are again becoming more accessible to individual investors. Firms are now increasingly able to compete not simply on price and quality, but also on their ability to provide "real-world" products and services. And this is done while offering social solutions as well.

All of this is happening despite the fact that most business schools today are not teaching, let alone emphasizing, the social response component that is emerging in today's capitalism. With some important exceptions, they are still focused on teaching the "money people" how to make more money . . . at the expense of higher and more important values. Another class of investors— from social response investors to billionaires like Warren Buffet and Michael Bloomberg—are also capitalizing on these new ESG principles.

With that said, let us use the same principles to find the most reliable data to set your own investment strategies in motion. We can begin with an overview of the evolution of ESG investing.

ESG METRICS AND SOCIALLY RESPONSIVE INVESTING

In its report on "US Sustainable, Responsible and Impact Investing Trends 2014," the Forum for Sustainable Investment and Responsible Investing made clear just how complex the responsible investing space has become:

> What's in a name? ESG, Ethical, Green, Impact, Mission, Responsible, Socially Responsible, Sustainable and Values are all labels that investors apply today to their strategies to consider environmental, social and corporate governance criteria to generate long-term competitive financial returns and positive societal impact. While the variety of labels can sometimes be confusing, the core message is clear. A growing number of investors, institutions and financial professionals are deploying and managing capital to build a more sustainable and equitable economy.

Simply put, there are a lot of names for what has come to stand for a very understandable and useful way to manage your money.

Until the last decade of the twentieth century, what had come to be known as socially responsible investing (SRI) set the standard for individuals and money managers who wanted to invest in companies that were sensitive to environmental, social, and governance issues. SRI investing emerged in the late 1960s and '70s in response to the growing public awareness of important social issues. It was a period that saw rioting in U.S. cities against racial discrimination, strong opposition to such international concerns as South African apartheid, and anti-war demonstrations against the country's involvement in the Vietnam War.

A growing awareness of environmental pollution also began to take hold. With events such as the discovery of toxic chemicals in the landfills of New York's Love Canal community, and the Cuyahoga River in northeastern Ohio catching fire in 1969, pollution was an issue that was hard to ignore. Even singer-songwriter Randy Newman celebrated the debris-fueled fire in his song "Burn On."

In response to these and other issues, people who were committed to SRI investing began using the marketplace to make their feelings known. By boycotting products and services of socially irresponsible companies, they made their voices heard and their values known, all in an effort to advance their causes. By the mid-1990s, investments driven by SRI considerations amounted to some $640 billion.

In the meantime, what many see as a competing investment philosophy emerged in the form of ESG investing. While both SRI and ESG investors believed in corporate social responsibility, they also differed in one primary way: SRI advocates tended to *avoid* investing in companies that were socially irresponsible. On the other hand, ESG investors sought to *identify* those companies that adhered to socially responsive values and made them part of their financial portfolios.

ESG analysts and investors became focused on searching for

data that enabled them to integrate ESG metrics into company profiles. They could then analyze the company's financial performance to determine if and to what degree its ESG commitment affected the bottom line, positively or negatively.

Unlike SRI investors, ESG investors used the data to improve the financial performance of their investments. They recognized that, while there is something to be said about restricting investments based on responsibility principles, it is more important—and more productive—to find ways in which ESG principles could be used to the investor's benefit. And while traditional investors focused on short-term financial performance as the key criterion for making decisions, ESG investors tended to take a longer-term view, often looking years down the road, to insure the financial sustainability of their investments.

It's not only the private investment community that has taken up the ESG cause. In 2006, the United Nations released a document titled "Principles for Responsible Investment," which has become known as PRI. This document formally recommended using ESG metrics as a basis for investments. Once the investments have been made, investors are encouraged to take an activist stance in promoting the ESG principles and practices of those companies. To give you a sense of how important the principles put forth in this document have become, some 1,335 organizations and professionals, including asset owners, investment managers, and professional service partners, have signed on to PRI.

Jane Ambachtsheer, a partner at Mercer Investments, heads its Global Responsible Investment team of consultants. She also served as a consultant to the United Nations during the creation of the PRI. In 2011, Jane became the recipient of the Social Investment Organization's Canadian SRI Lifetime Achievement Award. She understands the growth of responsible investing very directly. In her words:

[t]he amount of activity and reading is snowballing. There is new research, new product in different asset classes and regions and issues of integration. There's a lot of opportunities, a lot of push, pull, it's a moving beast.

She emphasizes that asset owners—and their advisors—have a great deal of work ahead of them. They must determine how they wish to allocate their investment dollars, assess their risk tolerance, and calculate the impact of ESG metrics and the regulatory environment on their investment choices. She expresses hope for the future because, as she points out, the 2008 financial crisis could have marked a severe deterrent to the rise of ESG investing. Instead, as she explains, "it was embraced. The ship has turned towards ESG integration; it is a slow moving ship, but it's hard to turn."

Other emerging evidence indicates that the data representing ESG metrics is not only increasingly integrated into company profiles, but also becoming positive indicators of a company's likely success. Deutsche Bank is one of the most fervent advocates for the inclusion of ESG metrics into its corporate practices, as the following statement indicates:

In its corporate banking business, Deutsche Bank fosters sustainability through measures such as providing financing and advisory services to support the growth of low-carbon businesses and sustainable energy projects. In 2013, the Bank supported renewable-energy projects with a total volume of more than USD 3.6bn and a generating capacity of more than 1,185 megawatts. In retail banking, the introduction and implementation of the FairShare™ concept means that the Bank's advisors are required to offer solutions that benefit clients and shareholders equally. Meanwhile, interest in investment products that integrate ESG factors has continued to grow in 2013. In Deutsche Asset & Wealth Management, a newly formed ESG Head Office is not only responsible for the implementation of a new ESG investment strategy, but also for the coordination, development and strengthening of ESG investment capabilities.

The effect of the ESG push has been profound. The proof can be found in the market share that ESG investors now command. The $640 billion in SRI investments in the mid-1990s had grown to $3.07 trillion in ESG investments by 2010, and had reached $3.74 trillion by 2012. The 2012 number represented more than 11 percent of the $33.3 trillion in total U.S. assets under management. Only two years later, the Forum for Sustainable and Responsible Investment (US SIF) reported that the total of SRI/ESG assets under management had grown to $6.57 trillion, up $2.83 trillion, or more than 75 percent, over the 2012 total. That increase meant that nearly 17 percent of the more than $38 trillion in assets under management were invested in ESG companies and funds by 2014.

NAVIGATING THE WORLD OF ESG INVESTMENTS

The positive influence of ESG metrics in the world of investing is significant. With the emergence of two investment organizations, MSCI and Bloomberg, as leading ratings agencies in the ESG space, for the first time, investors can measure the success of this new trend against investment failures since 2008. And this can be done based on a set of measurable criteria without bias or ideology. Investors can now answer the question: "Is investing in companies based on ESG metrics less risky than investments based on speculative capitalism?"

The answer is "yes."

One of the most important players in this movement is the nonprofit organization Ceres. As discussed in Chapter 2, Ceres was formed by forty-seven leading agencies of the social responsibility investing community. It was formed to provide an avenue for greater shareholder input in letting companies know the importance of including ESG metrics in many of its decisions. When companies are engaged in such activities as changing their products, repositioning production and distribution strategies, or increasing growth globally, the newly formed Ceres group felt that shareholder input should be included in that process. At the time of its founding, Ceres' purpose was: To create a reliable although narrow avenue for greater shareholder input into the destinies of companies.

Since then, the popularity of ESG metrics—the growing awareness of what they stand for and what they mean to investors, customers, and clients—has widened what was once a narrow avenue into what is fast becoming a superhighway. Credit must be given to Ceres and SRI investors for initially creating the ESG path. Now, with Bloomberg and MSCI assuming a greater role in the ESG marketplace, investors are able to review risk data that was not previously accessible.

This responsible investing movement snuck in through the back door. It happened thanks to key agencies such as Bloomberg and MSCI that gradually began to include ESG data as part of the foundation of their recommendations. To help guide investors, they shared this informative data in reports and through other accessible outlets.

During the initial years of this movement, the investor's role in promoting ESG metrics was limited. Socially responsible investments accounted for less than 1 percent of the money invested in corporate stock. Today, some twenty years later, that percentage has increased to 17 percent. As MSCI and Bloomberg began to automate ESG metrics, these measures became recognized as integral components of the broader universe of investment criteria. Investors and investment managers discovered that firms were more competitive, more successful, and better able to compete for capital and talent if they followed ESG principles and practices.

The ESG data that now informs and changes the nature of risk data has essentially become a part of the investing toolbox . . . in many cases without analysts and brokers being aware of it. It has become a key component of the investment industry in a very unobtrusive, yet very effective way. The SRI innovators created the early inroads into approved investment strategy, and now the investment "machine" has incorporated their principles—principles that have become an integral part of how risk is assessed in the financial world.

DATA GATHERERS

At his point, you are familiar with the individual components of the ESG metrics, and are aware of the concerns of companies and analysts who focus on this space. Bloomberg and MSCI, which have incorporated ESG metrics into their data capture and presentation models, offer a somewhat reduced version of those metrics. It is important to understand that both companies capture and analyze tens of millions of data sets when they pull together snapshots of the ESG-related policies and practices of different firms. It would be impossible for individual investors or smaller investment brokerages to even begin to collect and analyze this amount of data. Thanks to Bloomberg, MSCI, and many other asset managers (see listing beginning on page 159), both brokers and individual investors now have this information at their fingertips.

Meaning of the
Environmental Metric

For the past twenty years, regulating the flow of carbon into the atmosphere by companies that release excessive greenhouse gases was perceived as an impossible challenge. It was feared that reducing their emission would also reduce the amount of available carbon-based fuels, which would then skyrocket in cost. In turn, this would negatively impact these companies, which are the very backbone of the economy.

The importance of the environmental metric is based on the fact that we live in a carbon- and a capital-constrained world. The solutions to two of the key investing issues we face—the problem of climate change and the excesses of speculative capitalism—are one in the same: heightened efficiency. In Chapter 2, you saw how several important companies have made energy efficiency an important component of their operating philosophy. The same new world companies that are the focus of this book are going to be the companies that warrant greater investor dollars than their less efficient competitors. Regarding the environmental metric, they are the companies that have found or are striving to find ways to reduce their carbon emissions into the atmosphere and manage waste in an effective manner.

With regard to incorporating the environmental metric into their data capture, analysis, and presentation of different companies, one of the key elements Bloomberg and MSCI look at is the company's *carbon emissions report*. Along with information about its carbon emissions, does the report include what the company is doing to reduce them? In addition, Bloomberg and MSCI look at waste reduction, as well as spilling and dumping violations as measures of responsible environmental policy.

Meaning of the Social Metric

The social set of metrics is always rapidly changing. It is difficult for corporations to react to these ceaselessly changing expectations. New world companies, however, respond to this diversity of social requests quite well.

The social metric data that is researched and reported by Bloomberg and MSCI involves four established main components. They are human rights violations, inappropriate labor practices, trade violations, and product liability issues.

If there are any UN or nation-state petitions citing human rights violations, they are factored into the MSCI social metric. They are also baked into Bloomberg's. The stock analysts at both organizations, and at most asset-management firms, have clear ways of defining what constitutes inappropriate labor practices or social actions. They do not focus deeply on matters such as wage disputes. Instead, they maintain a bigger picture of social risks to ferret out mismanagement. In addition, they look at national and international trade violations as part of this metric, as well as the entire register of product liability violations and legal affairs.

Meaning of the Governance Metric

Although both Bloomberg and MSCI have significantly simplified their presentations of governance information, they still offer an enormous amount of data. One of the sources they use is the Global Reporting Initiative (GRI), which includes nearly 250 variables. All of the data is included, but it is presented in a condensed, coherent manner to be useful to investors. Among the governance components addressed by Bloomberg and MSCI include executive misconduct, which consists of scandalous activity rather than executive overpayment, and an assessment of the independence of a company's Board of Directors.

Thanks to the breadth, depth, and availability of this data in a usable format, we are capable of achieving what was once an impossible level of transparency. We are now more capable of looking deeply into corporate policies and practices and incorporating what we discover into our investment decisions.

WEIGHING THE EVIDENCE

Investors and investment managers also have an increasing bank of evidence regarding the effectiveness of incorporating ESG metrics into their investment strategy. The evidence is not anecdotal, nor is it based on hearsay. Quite the contrary. It is strongly supported by an increasing body of academic research and industry evidence. What follows are a few examples of the rapidly increasing evidence in favor of using the principles of social response capitalism as a basis for successful investing.

A 2012 study involving over 160 research projects was conducted by Deutsche Bank Climate Advisors. And it produced some startling outcomes. According to their financial results, companies with high ESG performance ratings overwhelmingly outperformed their fellow companies that did not rank high. The academic studies, which made up about two-thirds of the projects examined, agreed that companies with high ratings for corporate social responsibility (CSR) and ESG factors have a lower cost of capital in terms of both debt (loans and bonds) and equity. Based on the results of its review, Deutsche Bank recommended that "ESG analysis should be built into the investment process of every serious investor, and into the corporate strategy of companies that care about shareholder value."

Another Deutsche Bank study, "The Impact of a Corporate Culture of Sustainability on Corporate Behavior and Performance" was conducted over an eighteen-year period from 1993 to

2011. The study monitored the differences between ninety companies with strong sustainability policies and practices and ninety companies with low sustainability standards. The conclusions were eye-opening: "High Sustainability firms dramatically outperformed the Low Sustainability ones in terms of both stock market and accounting measures . . . in the long term." The annual above-market average return for the high-sustainability sample was 4.8 percent higher than for their counterparts and with lower volatility. The high-sustainability companies also performed much better as measured by returns on both equity and assets.

The study also reached other important conclusions. It discovered that corporations that have voluntarily adopted ESG metrics as an important part of their approach to doing business "represent a fundamentally distinct type of the modern corporation." The study found that awareness of "sustainability" as an important component of corporate management has grown in the past twenty years from almost nothing to a "dominant theme today." In addition, responsible corporations pay more attention to the well-being of their employees, customers, and shareholders than to non-ESG companies.

In another example, the California Public Employees' Retirement System's governance focus list was concerned with the weak performance of the companies in which it had invested. During a three-year period, CalPERS' investments in those companies, whose corporate philosophies *did not* include sustainability, produced cumulative returns averaging 39 percent below their benchmark. When the group shifted its investment strategy to include sustainability-responsive companies, the returns during the next five years were 17 percent above their benchmark.

The change in investment philosophy that brought about the dramatic turnaround in the fund's performance is articulated in a CalPERS white paper. The organization described its position on environmental risk this way: "We recognize that rising demand for food and resources globally, coupled with the likely effects of climate change, will have a potential impact on risk-adjusted returns." Regarding governance, the report stated: "The alignment of interests between investors and managers is vitally important." In the area of social issues, it said, "How a company treats its employees, its reputation in the community and issues like human rights in global supply chains can present risks and also opportunities."

There's more evidence in favor of ESG metrics. In a document titled "The Financial Performance of SRI Funds Between 2002 and 2009," study authors Olaf Weber and Marco Mansfield found this:

> [T]he SRI [Social Response Investing] fund portfolio reached a significantly higher return than MSCI World Index. Furthermore with respect to the financial performance of SRI funds, the weight of the financial rating of the funds was positive while the weight of the sustainability rating was negative. Thus an in-depth financial analysis of SRI funds helps to identify those funds performing financially well.

Specifically, the report states that "MSCI World shows a lower return compared to the mean of the SRI funds" during what is described as "the bull phase" of the time period studied. During this time, the return on SRI investments was 40.4 percent higher; in other words, "the portfolio of SRI funds shows a significantly higher financial return [than] the MSCI World Index."

Regarding the link between "corporate sustainability and financial performance," a report by RobecoSAM, an investment specialist with exclusive focus on sustainability investing, said:

> The results of its [RobecoSAM's] quantitative analysis on the correlation between these two factors reveal that from

2001 to 2010, sustainability leaders deliver an average out-performance of 1.74 percent per annum with a positive information ratio of 0.53. This demonstrates the alpha potential of integrating SAM's proprietary sustainability research into traditional financial analysis.

To translate, the term "alpha potential" refers to the "risk ratio" of a company's return to investors when compared to such conventional measures as the Capital Asset Pricing Model (CAPM). The CAPM measures the predicted rate of return of a company's stock based on the risk premium of the investment when it is compared with a similar equity in a hypothetical risk-free environment. If a company's alpha potential—when compared to a similar company in a risk-free environment—is positive, then the stock is a good buy. If the alpha potential is negative, then analysts and brokers recommend against investing in it.

In the RobecoSAM study, the alpha potential of responsible ESG firms is at +1.74, a very healthy positive measure. It means that, despite their risk ratios, the stocks of these companies significantly outperform the market when measured against companies in a no-risk environment. High ESG scores indicate the likelihood of a company performing strongly.

In short, all of these social developments help investors gain insight into companies. The new world companies featured in this book provide them with the confidence that their investments will be solid and compounding.

CONCLUSION

While the ESG strides made by Bloomberg and MSCI have helped us become much more enlightened and responsible investors, there is still work to be done, still more you can do to refine your investment approach.

We are fighting a long-term battle here, both on the investment side and on the social response side. On the investment side, while the money-focused companies and advisors zoom in on next quarter's numbers, the social response companies focus on the next generation—on issues that are far more important in the long term. As it turns out, these longer-term concerns are actually much better predictors of a firm's prospects for success. And equally if not more important, they encourage the global economy to thrive and benefit all of the planet's citizens in the most responsible way.

Again, while the world's countries are still operating on the nation-state model, its major corporations are abandoning the speculative capitalism that is the corporate equivalent of the nation-state model. New world companies are moving toward social response capitalism, which takes into account that the people of this world are now united in ways that were unimaginable even only a decade ago. This emerging movement is possible thanks to the rapidly advancing globalization of the economy and, as a result, of our social and business consciousness.

The focus of this chapter has been on advancing investor awareness of the benefits of socially responsive companies. While responding to the needs of people throughout the world, these companies are also combating the excesses and corruption associated with speculative capitalism.

This chapter has encouraged you to become more proactive in your investments. Rather than giving up complete control to your broker, become an ESG partner in managing your portfolio. The good news is that many money managers are now beginning to factor in these metrics before recommending investment options to clients. ESG metrics have become more than another way to assess risk factors: They are actually predictors of companies' long-term success. And for that reason, they should play an important role in how you structure your investment portfolio.

Following ESG principles as you develop and manage your portfolio offers a much better chance of investment success. Of course, this is not to say that you won't find success if you ignore ESG metrics. After all, as the saying goes, "Even a blind hog gets an acorn once in a while." But the facts are becoming clearer all the time: *You ignore ESG metrics at your own risk. Follow them if you want to significantly increase your long-term investing success.*

6

Engines of Freedom

The Model of
a New World Company

t's a fact. People throughout the world love their cars. And why not? Cars are engines of freedom—a significant part of life that allows us to get where we want to be. It goes without saying that in industrialized nations, the automobile has become a necessity in peoples' everyday lives. So it's no wonder that the auto industry is a major sector of today's global economy.

In 2014, automobile manufacturers produced some 83 million cars and trucks in thirty-nine different countries. To put that statistic into perspective, only twenty-three of the nearly two hundred countries in the world have populations greater than the number of cars produced worldwide each year. Currently, there are more than a billion vehicles in operation.

While it is true that we are dependent on cars, the increase in their use has led to a number of undesirable consequences, including a rise in traffic jams and highway accidents. Most disturbing, however, is that cars have become the primary contributor to one of the most dangerous conditions we face: environmental deterioration. Every day, auto exhaust fumes negatively impact the quality of the air we breathe. They are responsible for more than half of the atmospheric pollution in major cities and even more in places like Los Angeles, Beijing, and Tokyo, where the climate and topography encourage the creation of smog. Along with causing respiratory problems and other health issues, air pollution has also had an effect on many forms of agriculture and natural resources.

To help restrict the emission of pollutants, in the 1960s, the U.S. required the installation of catalytic converters in new cars. This helped reduce the amount of carbon monoxide, hydrocarbons, and nitrogen oxides into the atmosphere; however, it also caused an increase in carbon dioxide (CO_2) emissions, which are now believed to contribute to global warming.

The problems posed by the overuse of cars—or more accurately, the overuse of the wrong kind and size of car—go well beyond environmental deterioration. They can negatively affect our quality of life. Consider the tremendous number of deaths and injuries caused by traffic accidents. In addition to causing pain—both physical and psychological—they also cost us billions of dollars in insurance, medical care, and lost wages. Also consider that the number of people suffering from asthma—that's one out of every twelve Americans—continues to grow by leaps and bounds each year. And with it come billions of dollars in medical care. And that is just the tip of the iceberg. For new world companies, such statistics are no longer overlooked. Instead, they offer insights into competitive advantages in answer to social needs.

SOCIAL RESPONSE CAPITALISM AND THE AUTOMOTIVE INDUSTRY

The country's first generation of socially responsible cars was developed during the opening years of the twenty-first century. From more fuel-efficient engines to the growing number of hybrid vehicles to the appearance of electric cars, the automotive industry has started paying attention to several important considerations in the move toward social response capitalism. These considerations involve automotive performance, energy consumption, and environmental responsibility. In an important sense, these three areas are connected to each other. As each one also involves a number of specific issues, it is best to examine them separately. After taking a look at these areas, it is important to consider two additional issues: what needs to be done to improve the first generation of socially responsible cars and what it will take to push the movement forward.

Automobile Performance

American car buyers demand performance and safety—two characteristics that the first generation of environmentally responsible cars simply did not meet. With freeways crowded with oversized SUVs going seventy-plus miles per hour, consumers have been reluctant to accept compromises in the size and performance of the many trial social-response autos.

This is especially true of electric cars, including such models as the Chevrolet EV Spark Hatchback, the Nissan Leaf Hatchback, and the Fiat 500e Hatchback. The Chevy Volt, while electrically powered, also features a gasoline-fueled generator that kicks in to charge its battery while the car is being driven.

It is also true of the first generation of hybrid vehicles, which did not necessarily meet the performance expectations of American consumers. In fact, as succeeding generations of hybrid vehicles appear on the market, it is becoming clear that manufacturers are devoting less effort toward enhanced energy efficiency and pollution reduction, and more effort toward improved power and speed. This is all in an effort to attract U.S. buyers who want high-performance vehicles.

One of the reasons Americans are currently able to remain so focused on vehicle performance is due to the price of gasoline. Although the country has experienced substantial gas price increases in the past decade, the increase has not been dramatic enough, nor sustained long enough to make the cost of gas the most important determining factor when buying a car. This differs from much of the rest of the world, where, in most places, the price of a gallon of gasoline is more than double what we pay in America. In the U.S., despite the lingering post-2008 recession, there have been no serious economic incentives to put resource efficiency alone ahead of performance and safety.

Energy Consumption

How does the price of gas affect the second consideration in the auto manufacturer's move toward social responsiveness—energy consumption? Let me begin the answer with another question: "Will the market for fuel-efficient cars and cars that use alternative power sources continue to be relatively small?" The answer to this question can be found in the emerging markets in such countries as China and India.

In 2013, five Chinese governmental departments collectively issued stringent new standards making it mandatory for Chinese cars to use no more than 6.9 liters of fuel per 100 kilometers driven. By 2020, that number must be reduced to 5.0 liters (1.3 gallons) per 100 km. To translate—getting 100 kilometers (62 miles) per 6.9 liters (1.8 gallons) of fuel translates to a little over 34 miles per gallon (mpg). By 2020, that number will jump to around 47 mpg. At the time of this announcement, the price of gasoline in China was equivalent to the U.S. cost of $6.50 per gallon.

You may be asking yourself, "Why do I care about China's fuel economy standards?" China is the largest automobile-producing country in the world and has more cars on the road than any other country on the planet. Of the nearly 83 million cars that were manufactured and sold worldwide in 2013, approximately 21 million were produced in China. That's more than 25 percent! As a means of comparison, in the same year, the United States, which is the second largest auto market in the world, produced just under 15 million cars, about three quarters of the number manufactured in China.

Fuel prices also drive the need for fuel efficiency in European cars. In most European countries, drivers pay the U.S. equivalent of about $8.00 per gallon of petrol. Given the evidence just presented, it's clear that the market for fuel-efficient cars is going to grow enormously in the coming decades. All new world companies understand this. In fact, firms like Flex, CAT, Toyota, and others mentioned in this book take advantage of higher fuel costs by offering more efficient products and solutions.

Environmental Responsibility

The third key factor for social response-driven automobile companies lies in their focus on the environment. In a recent study conducted by Wirthlin Worldwide, 80 percent of Americans responding to a questionnaire held the opinion that "increased investment in public transportation would . . . reduce . . . air pollution, and save energy." I believe this is a strong indication that Americans feel auto manufacturers are not devoting enough of their resources toward improving fuel efficiency, nor do they trust the industry to help solve environmental problems.

So what can the auto industry do to reduce its negative impact on the environment? One answer can be seen in Toyota's hybrid cars, which came out in 1997 and was specifically designed to reduce emissions and increase mileage. To accomplish these goals, Toyota designed a parallel hybrid powertrain system. Figure 6.1 on page 138 shows the impact that this system has had on the environment. A hybrid fleet of 7 million releases 49 million fewer tons of carbon dioxide emissions into the atmosphere.

It is estimated that air pollution is responsible for the premature deaths of some 200,000 people in the United States each year. And "vehicle emissions are the biggest contributor to these premature deaths." The only other source of particulates released into the atmosphere that is even close to auto emissions is from the generation of electricity.

Before the introduction of Toyota's hybrid vehicles, the auto industry's efforts to be more environmentally friendly were not

CARBON: GLOBAL FLEET REDUCTIONS
7 MILLION

49 MILLION FEWER TONS OF CO$_2$ EMISSIONS

Figure 6.1. The Hybrid Powertrain Factor

Thanks to Toyota's hybrid powertrain system, a hybrid fleet of 7 million releases 49 million fewer tons of carbon dioxide emissions into the atmosphere.

fully rooted in social response product development (SRPD). Rather, they were characterized by old-fashioned corporate philanthropy, such as donating to popular causes. This was coupled with a dim awareness of a possible market for more fuel-efficient and alternative-fuel based vehicles. In other words, most automakers served their markets with a twentieth-century world view.

One top priority of U.S. auto companies is their spending on advertising. In recent years, some $10 billion are spent annually on television ads. That works out to nearly $700 for every car sold. And if you watch TV at all, no doubt you have noticed that car commercials rarely focus on the need for environmentally responsible vehicles.

And yet, in spite of this, the automotive industry has always perceived itself as innovative. It also sees itself as providing more jobs, more freedom, and more wealth than any other business, despite the billions of dollars it spends on advertising and the billions more it devotes to purchase incentives and discounts.

DRIVING THE MARKET TOWARD SOCIAL RESPONSE PRODUCT DEVELOPMENT

For a company to take the lead in introducing and spreading social response capitalism in the automotive market requires vision, leadership, and a great deal of guts—the same qualities that characterize the great leaders of the Western world. It must combine the vision of an Abraham Lincoln, the courage and fortitude of a Winston Churchill, and the leadership of a Dwight David Eisenhower.

It is not by accident that I have chosen these specific leaders who rose to greatness by answering the challenges of war. They characterize what is needed to lead the charge toward more responsible policies and practices in the twenty-first century automotive business. Any company in the auto industry that rises to the challenge of social responsiveness must be ready to do battle with powerful forces.

The challenge is in taking a leap into the future that incorporates the things that are not so subtly diminishing our quality of life. Social response capitalists develop superior cars, computers, and buildings to drive the new world markets.

ENTER TOYOTA

The Toyota story began more than a century ago with Henry Ford's creation of the Ford Motor Company. With it, Ford launched the revolutionary idea of the mass production of automobiles that changed car manufacturing—and, by extension, society—forever. Henry Ford's story was the primary source of inspiration for Japanese businessman Eiji Toyoda. When Eiji's cousin Kiichiro Toyoda built an automobile factory, he asked Eiji, who had just graduated with an engineering degree in 1936, to work with him. This production facility would eventually become the Toyota Motor Corporation.

Initially, Eiji Toyoda's role in the company was to use the American drive for production efficiency as a model and develop a manufacturing process that used a reduced amount of materials for its automobiles. During his time as president and later CEO of the company, Toyoda brought into being a global empire that is now characterized by clean, efficient production practices that have reduced the environmental footprint of its manufacturing processes, as well as of the automobiles it builds. What Mr. Ford did for auto manufacturing in the early twentieth century, Mr. Toyoda did for the industry in the second half of the century.

Toyota made its inauspicious entry into the American market in 1957 when it introduced the American public to one of its most successful car models—the Toyopet Crown (see Figure 6.2 below).

The Toyopet was well-suited for Japan, but it did not meet the U.S. market conditions and expectations. In addition to being too small for American drivers, it was underpowered and uncomfortable. The car's fuel efficiency was not much of a selling feature in the United States, where the cost of gasoline—about 25 cents a

Figure 6.2. The Toyopet Crown

Although well-suited for Japan, the Toyopet Crown was not able to compete in the U.S. market.

gallon—was not a cause for concern. The Toyopet was also less sophisticated than the American models and not as reliable. The U.S. auto industry, which had been in existence for nearly five decades, produced cars that reflected the latest manufacturing advances and a relentless marketing strategy. The still-fledgling Japanese company could not compete.

From this failed experience, Toyota realized that to compete in the U.S. market, it had to better understand the desires of American drivers. It meant building cars that served a market where comfort and reliability reigned supreme. Before launching any additional models, the company made a number of innovative changes, including:

- The development of a new "lean manufacture" process. Based on Henry Ford's original mass production model, this modified system produced cars using less metal, paint, and plastic than the competitors. It reduced the cost of the cars and saved resources.

- The introduction of a line of cars that, in addition to offering the same level of comfort found in U.S. cars, was of higher quality and demanded fewer repairs.

- The marketing of a brand that was attractive to a younger generation of buyers—consumers who did not feel the same loyalty to U.S. cars as the earlier generation of pre-World War II Americans.

Toyota's first break in its battle for American approval came about with the oil crisis of the 1970s, when the cost of fuel rose dramatically. The fuel economy of the still-new Japanese brand allowed Toyota to seize the efficiency initiative from U.S. automakers. The change was profound. Americans began shifting from what *Harper's* magazine writer William Tucker called "dinosaurs in our driveways" to the more efficient cars offered by its Japanese competitors. It forced General Motors, Ford, and Chrysler to reconsider the qualities of their cars.

This began Toyota's three-decade journey toward becoming the world-class manufacturer of mobile transport technology it is today. The company radically reduced its cycle time for developing new car models from thirty-six to twenty-four months. This gave Toyota the competitive advantage of being able to respond to shifts in demand in about one-third the time it took for its American competitors to accomplish the same. In short, it has learned to be responsive to new world urgencies better than any auto manufacturer on earth.

Instead of looking backward to determine product development strategies, Toyota anticipated market requirements by looking ahead. This enabled it to build brands and create production capacity and inventory based on what it saw as future demands. This strategic revolution provided Toyota with a blueprint for moving toward a socially responsible business model—one that today has become the best in the world.

The Toyota Blueprint

Toyota is one of the leading examples of a company that had the foresight to incorporate social response into its business model. It created what can be considered the blueprint for how multinational companies can incorporate social response principles in the form of environmental responsibility and manufacturing efficiency into its products. This is the heart of social response product development.

Toyota's business model has placed it at the top of an important global industry that could very well be one of the keys to our collective long-term survival. The transportation industry must be a leader in improving the quality of the air we breathe, while at the same time developing new, cleaner renewable sources of fuel.

Hiroshi Okuda, former president of Toyota Industries, chairman of Toyota Motor Corporation, and president of Japan Bank for International Cooperation, has summed up Toyota's perspectives in this way:

> I do not believe environmental protection and economic growth are mutually exclusive. Economic growth that ignores environmental consequences is in my view reckless, but on the other hand, attempting to resolve global environmental issues without recognizing the need for economic growth is unrealistic. I believe our objective should be sustainable growth.

Combining environmental sustainability with economic growth, as articulated by Okuda, is at the foundation of what is shaping new world companies today.

The Hybrid Truth

As previously mentioned, one of the primary reasons for Toyota's trip to the top of the list of auto companies is that it has focused on pioneering new models and technology by looking forward, not backward. At the same time, it has maintained high manufacturing and product standards. The prime example of Toyota's leadership in actually exceeding environmental standards can be found in its gasoline-electric hybrid vehicle, the Prius. From its introduction into the global marketplace in 2000, the Prius put Toyota in the driver's seat where fostering environmental excellence in transportation is concerned. Even the Prius' name—derived from the Latin word meaning "before"—was a sign that the company was sending a message that it was "way ahead" of the curve in its development of this vehicle.

The creation of this environmentally friendly car has made Toyota the very model of a socially responsive company. It shows what a company can achieve when it takes its eye off the price-profit prize and expands its focus toward sustainability and social good in developing its products. As shown in Figure 6.3 below, Toyota's sustainability focus involves more than its manufacturing process. It also involves reaching out to suppliers and dealers—

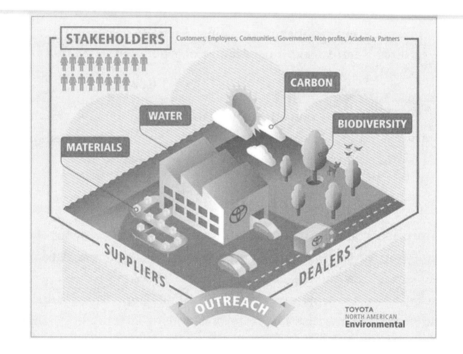

Figure 6.3. Toyota's Sustainability Focus

This graphic, designed by Toyota, reflects the company's strategic view and the mission it wishes to accomplish at its manufacturing sites and North American headquarters. It shows the company's commitment to the environment by reducing its use of water and materials, and by lessening its impact on our land and atmosphere. It also identifies its stakeholders—customers, staff, and the communities in which it has sites—who all have a say in its future.

the companies it partners with—as well as its stakeholders, to promote its ESG values and practices.

Toyota's purpose in developing its hybrid had nothing to do with improving its image among consumers (not that it had anything against good public relations). Its product strategy involved the reading of future public needs. This allowed the company to anticipate and build long-term markets for its products. Like all companies, Toyota wants to make a profit. And it does not view the anticipation of public needs a philanthropic distraction from doing so. Rather, it embraces this step toward social responsiveness as a key to its ultimate success.

The years 2010 through 2014 were pivotal in liberating Toyota's hybrid powertrain family of cars. Senior management used the following numbers in its decision to continue the company's effort. At the end of 2013, Toyota had the three top-selling hybrid cars on the market. Its Prius (117, 626 sold), Camry Hybrid (21,466 sold), and Lexus CT Hybrid (8,647 sold). Collectively, these three cars outsold the other six non-Toyota hybrids put together. And the Toyota models didn't just outsell them; they outsold them by a 4 to 1 ratio! Toyota also had the number six car on the list—the Lexus RX Hybrid. The U.S. market reflects only a small fraction of Toyota's dominance in the alternative-fuel vehicles market.

By 2014, the cumulative worldwide sales of Toyota hybrid vehicles since the introduction of the Prius in 2000 topped 6 million units. Based on this milestone, Toyota described its corporate philosophy in words that demonstrate the meaning of social response capitalism:

> Helping mitigate the environmental effects of vehicles is a priority at Toyota. Based on its belief that environment-friendly vehicles can only truly have a positive impact if they

are widely used, Toyota has endeavored to encourage the mass-market adoption of hybrid vehicles.

Currently, the company manufactures twenty-four different models of its hybrid cars, which are sold in eighty countries throughout the world—and it isn't stopping there. Toyota recently announced that it will be launching fifteen new hybrid models by 2017.

Of the top ten hybrid and electric vehicles sold in the United States, only two American cars made the grade: the Ford Fusion and the Chevy Volt. Together, these two cars sold fewer than 11,000 units in the first half of 2012.

The trends described above helped show Toyota that it could accelerate and take advantage of continued sales from 2012 and beyond. As two industry analysts put it, "If the market for alternative energy vehicles does indeed pick up, American car manufacturers will be behind." And I would add, the strategic development of environmentally friendly cars represents an enterprise on which the survival of our planet now depends.

FROM THE "CORPORATE ELITE"
TO THE "CORPORATE COMMUNITY"

At one time, corporate executives in the auto industry were considered members of an elite group—a view that is rapidly disappearing. Gone are the days when top executives and board members are able to avoid addressing environmental issues and the needs of people—both consumers who buy cars and the workers who actually produce them. In the "good old days," the corporate culture of the automotive industry was dominated by these corporate officers.

In my opinion, one person who represented the trend of top-down dominance was Harley Earl—the head designer for General Motors during the mid-1900s. I would describe Earl as "the tyrant of the tailfin" and the man who brought the two-year lifespan of each new car model into being. Under his guidance, GM produced a line of cars that had what we now see as exotic design and the need for speed as the primary reasons for being. This period in automotive development is seen as one of the most decadent in the history of the American automobile.

Figure 6.4 below shows Earl's tailfin design on the back of the 1959 Cadillac—one of the cars that represent his legacy. Such designs were conceived behind the closed doors of corporate executives, away from any outside influences that might have represented concerns beyond those of the corporate directors themselves. Boardroom focus was on decadent "shiny new toy" designs, big-engine delivery, and profit. And while innovation is certainly an important part of automotive design, before the emergence of social responsibility as an important component of innovation, tailfins and chrome reigned for many years as the guiding principles in this corporate fiefdom.

By contrast, as Toyota evolved into a dominant force in the automotive industry, corporate leadership broadened to include

**Figure 6.4.
The 1959 Cadillac Tailfin**

Designs such as the tailfin were produced during what has been considered one the most decadent periods of automotive development.

not only company executives, but also company engineers, designers, production worker reps, and financial planners, to mention a few. They all worked together—and continue to work together—to develop products that address issues such as their effects on the global climate, on local and regional air pollution, and on the conservation of natural resources.

The technology that Toyota developed as it designed and built the first hybrid vehicles will give you a sense of why it has become the world leader in the auto industry. By understanding that neither the gasoline engine nor the electric engine is the optimal answer for powering a car, Toyota developed its hybrid technology. The hybrid's electric engine powers the vehicle at lower speeds, replacing the gas engine, which is most inefficient and polluting at this speed. The gas engine kicks in at higher speeds, where the electric motor does not produce the power necessary to meet the higher-speed demands, such as those needed for freeway driving.

Toyota also found an additional way to make use of the car's electric motor. When the driver steps on the brake pedal, the electric motor turns into a generator that recharges the car's battery. This is testimony that the electronics in Toyota hybrids are incredibly sophisticated. They enable the car to make the most efficient use of the energy available, including the energy generated by applying the brakes. Toyota's technical innovation was combined with a revolution in the production process as the company refined its manufacturing approach.

Toyota's Total Production System

The Toyota Production System (TPS) is among the many reasons for the company's success. This system has the capability to detect abnormalities during the manufacturing/production process so that corrective action can be taken immediately. This quality-control feature is built into the production line, so the workers on the line (rather than a small cadre of quality-control professionals) can stop production as necessary to eliminate defects. This "total quality control" approach empowers the entire work force to prevent defects. In addition, finding and fixing defects immediately prevents waste in both time and resources.

TPS may be a product-centered solution, but it also produces person-centered benefits. It moves the management process out of the corporate executive offices and into the corporate community, vesting workers on the production lines with the shared responsibility of improving production efficiency and product quality of the cars they build. When production workers are involved and invested in the final product, they are more accountable in their jobs and proud of their work.

In the 1990s, Toyota's proposed strategies seemed highly questionable to many—nothing more than educated speculation. But the end results are now abundantly clear. Toyota was actually ahead of the new world curve. Significantly.

KNOWING WHO YOU ARE AND WHAT YOU REPRESENT

Much of my consulting on product positioning, emerging markets, and issues management is focused on helping corporate leaders and operational managers see clearly where they stand on matters of social responsiveness. Do they consider current social needs in their existing product base and in the development of new product lines? Are they planning to provide products that are not only ahead of their time, but ahead of the curve? Do they view themselves as leaders who are determined to develop products that their competitors, who may not share their foresight, will ultimately have to adopt?

Toyota is a prime example of a company that has done all of this. As it developed its long-term strategic plan, Toyota recognized that the automotive industry was increasingly driven by several factors: government mandates, social awareness, and the corresponding changes in market trends. Hybrids now represent more than 3 percent of the total cars sold in the United States. This is a clear indication of how Toyota's expansion of those in leadership positions enabled it to introduce products that were far ahead of the curve to a market that was just starting to become aware of that curve.

As Toyota maintains and further grows its position as the world's largest car manufacturer, its expertise in lean manufacturing and its product differentiation skills will help elevate the performance and social expectations of every associated market. This would include everything from automotive supply chains to major energy efficiency innovators like Flex and Siemens, who add further electronic efficiency to car performance.

Toyota' willingness to listen to social needs—and then respond incisively—is what has made the company a major force for good. It is an exemplary new world company that has made it clear that in the decades ahead, it will strive to maintain, even grow, its lead in in the areas of lean manufacture, social product innovation, and sustained value.

SOCIAL RESPONSE RISKS

Are there hidden risks associated with Toyota's hybrid-product family of vehicles? Some believe there are, but the risks are not hidden. One specific issue centers on the nickel metal hydride (NiMH) batteries that are used in hybrid gas-electric cars like the Toyota Prius. There is some concern that an influx of these batteries may result in a recycling and waste-disposal issue. Some critics have characterized this possibility as a ten-year sleeping giant. While this may be an emerging issue for hybrid car manufacturers to deal with, we need only look to the current disposal of conventional lead-acid auto batteries to offer a response.

The U.S. Environmental Protection Agency (EPA) estimates that 90 percent of the wet-cell lead-acid batteries used in standard cars are recycled by local retailers and service shops, as mandated by most state laws. Because NiMH batteries have recoverable amounts of nickel and cobalt, recycling them is a strong possibility. This is especially likely as the volume of these batteries increases with the growing sales of hybrid cars.

Refusing to adopt the Toyota model of social response capitalism can be a perilous decision—one that will almost inevitably consign your company to the ash-heap of corporate history. What remains most important, however, is for social response leaders to push ahead through the challenging gauntlet of environmental regulations, stakeholder concerns, and market pressures in order to move forward.

THE SOCIAL RESPONSE FUTURE IS NOW

The move toward hybrid cars is gradually being recognized as the truly important milestone it represents. This is seen not only in the development of the car itself, but also in meeting the needs of the people of the world.

Equally critical, is the growing importance of hybrid vehicles and the business model that Toyota has created for the introduction of hybrid technology. This represents an important step in the corporate world's understanding that social response capitalism and the principles and practices it embodies can be the foundation for real, principled growth of corporate entities. I strongly believe that it will replace the focus that is solely on profits. It is a change that will prove to be as financially beneficial as ignoring it will be dangerous.

Releasing a new type of vehicle into a traditional market was an incredibly high-risk move for Toyota. But with the introduction and subsequent refinement and success of the Toyota Prius, and with Toyota's ongoing development of hybrid versions of the company's ten core models, it appears to have superseded the dated products of many other car manufacturers. The histories of automotive corporations are littered with failures and outmoded vehicles, such as gas-guzzling SUVs, including GM's Hummer; diesel fuel-devouring commercial trucks; and European and Asian cars that remained dependent on the century-old internal combustion engine well beyond the time that it should have been discarded.

In my opinion, Toyota's adoption of the principles of social response capitalism was a courageous and important move. It means that sensitivity to social issues *must* be adopted to insure long-term success. From its beginnings as a "nice-to-have" component of corporate messaging, the principles and practices of social response capitalism have become "must-haves" for the assurance of company survival.

CONCLUSION

The principles of social response capitalism provide a model to follow, not simply for auto manufacturers, but for all companies throughout the world. And yet, the magnetic force toward making a quick buck continues to be the goal of many speculative corporations. There is certainly no question that a company's ability to survive in today's marketplace is no easy task. And showing a few profitable years is no guarantee of future success, especially over the coming decades. Without the principles of ESG metrics to follow, dwindling world resources coupled with growing consumer demands are among the very real threats to those corporations that are unprepared.

In the twenty-first century, businesses of all types owe it to themselves, their employees, their clients and customers, and the people of the world to embrace social response capitalism. It is no longer a matter of just going along with the flow; in a very real sense, it is a matter of survival for companies as well as for this world. As the population continues to increase, it is mission critical that new world companies teach us how to do more with less.

Conclusion

The Future of Social Response Capitalism

The nature of business is changing, and changing rapidly. At one time, the single driving force of every major corporation was making a profit—with little or no time to monitor the consequences of environmental, employee, or customer damage. Today, those consequences not only matter, they have become a driving force in how the most successful companies conduct their business. Where once multi-national corporations ruled the lands in which they operated, today, an increased awareness and sense of social responsiveness has given rise to companies of a new type—ones that bring innovation and sustained value to the countries in which they operate. The growth and profits of these new world companies come from their clear understanding of what people want and need, not just what they are willing to pay for.

Based on my experience as a business consultant for over thirty years, I have shared in this book some of my observations regarding the way businesses are beginning to be conducted throughout the world. One of the conclusions I have drawn is that the influence of new world companies can be just as powerful in improving the quality of the lives, perspectives, and health of the people on this earth than that of national governments. Maybe even more so.

Another more impactful conclusion I have reached involves investors. Investors can be quite astute at picking sustained winners. The way in which a corporation conducts its business in three areas—environmental concerns; social issues that affect people around the world; and the breadth, quality, and integrity of its governance team—is now key to the success and the sustenance of firms. To understand which businesses are more likely to enjoy long-term success, I have relied increasingly on data that measures a firm's adherence to ESG values. This criteria acts as a more reliable yardstick to gauge which companies are most likely to grow and prosper in the coming decades.

By knowing what questions to ask, investors can work with their financial advisers to gain an advantage when selecting their investment. When you take into account how a company complies with ESG values and practices, not only will you be putting your money into a better run company, you will also be investing in a better future for yourself, your family, and the world. Beginning on page 159, you will find an extensive list of asset managers that focus on investments in new world companies—companies that I believe uphold the very principles discussed in this book.

Whether you work with a financial advisor or you do your own investing, it is important to point out that the stock markets of today are prone to rises and dips. And these ups and downs can sometimes make investing seem like a ride on a rollercoaster. These rocky performances are often caused by geopolitics, today's news headlines, and speculative investors "playing" the market. While new world company shares are tied to these forces that influence the markets, in the long run, it is my feeling that they will outperform other companies.

I believe that new world companies are significant representatives of positive change in our world of seven billion souls. Every trend explored in this book suggests that they are a force for social good.

These companies share what I see as three critically important characteristics. First, they incorporate socially responsible values into their business models, and they extend those values around the globe. Second, they have brought customers, employees, and key stakeholders at every level into the decision-making process, effectively democratizing the way they conduct their affairs. Finally, they are committed to long-term growth and sustainability. They build and consolidate their positions as the arbiters of a values-based way of doing business. Although still in an early stage of development, this "new world" manner of doing business is on its way to becoming a permanent force for good.

Asset Managers
With Focus on ESG Metrics

The following table provides an abbreviated list of asset management companies that support investing based on ESG principles. Included are brief descriptions of the firms and the amount of money managed by each.

Fund Management Companies	Description	Assets Under Management ($ in billions)
Acadian Asset Management	Specializes in active global and international equity strategies; employs sophisticated analytical models for active stock selection.	$65
Adams Street Partners, LLC	Global private equity investment management firm; focuses on long-term, sustainable investment success.	$22.4
Bentall Kennedy	Largest real estate investment advisors in North America; also Canada's largest property manager.	$31
BlackRock	World's largest asset management firm.	$4,720 ($4.72 trillion)

Fund Management Companies	Description	Assets Under Management ($ in billions)
Boston Common Asset Management	Employee-owned; leader in global sustainability initiatives.	$2
Boston Trust & Investment Management/Walden Asset Management	Boston Trust's Walden Asset Management division is a leader in the sustainable and responsible investment (SRI) industry.	$7.9 (Boston Trust) $2.7 (Walden)
Breckinridge Capital Advisors	Specializes in fixed income portfolios; provides access to sustainability bonds.	$20.2
Calvert Investments	Global leader in responsible and sustainable investing.	$13.5
Cartica Capital	Investment manager of emerging markets.	$2
CBRE Global Investors	Global leader in real estate investment management.	$88.4
ClearBridge Investments	Equities investment manager; integrates ESG analysis into its fundamental research platform.	$116.8
Domini Social Investments	Woman-owned and managed investment firm; specializes in socially responsible investing.	$31.3
Global Environment Fund	Global investor in middle market companies dedicated to the energy, environmental, and natural resources sectors.	$1
Goldman Sachs Asset Management (GSAM)	Asset management arm of Goldman Sachs Group. Its Global Responsible Equity Portfolio factors ESG criteria to determine responsible and sustainable investments.	$1,150 ($1.15 trillion)
Great Lakes Advisors	Manages socially responsible and environmentally sustainable governance investments.	$5
Miller Howard Investments	Committed to socially responsible ESG investments; employee-owned.	$9.1
Nelson Capital Management	Employs socially responsible investment strategies.	$2.03
Northern Trust Asset Management	Global leader in innovative investment management.	$946

Fund Management Companies	Description	Assets Under Management ($ in billions)
Parnassus Investments	Independent, employee-owned investment manager; factors ESG criteria into investment decisions.	$12.7
Pax World Investments	Pioneer in the sustainable investment industry; uses full integration of ESG factors into investment decisions.	$2.5
PIMCO	Global investment manager of mutual funds and bonds that utilize ESG as part of investment analysis.	$1,520 ($1.52 trillion)
Portfolio 21 Investments	Global equity mutual fund with sole ESG focus; merged with Trillium Asset Management.	$0.59
Principal Global Investors	Committed to responsible investing and ESG issues; subsidiary of Principal Financial Group.	$311
Prudential Real Estate Investors	Global real estate investment business of Prudential Financial.	$61.7
Quotient Investors	Equity fund fully utilizing ESG factors; selected for California Public Employees Retirement System (CalPERS).	$0.46
Rock Creek Group	Global investment and advisory firm with a commitment to serving local and global communities; has long history of working on ESG issues.	$7
Satori Capital, LLC	Private equity firm based on sustainable approaches; focuses primarily on family- or entrepreneur-owned companies.	$1.2
State Street Global Advisors (SSgA)	World's second largest asset manager; the investment management division of State Street Corp.; offers green bond strategy products.	$2,421 ($2.42 trillion)
TIAA–CREF (Teachers Insurance and Annuity Assn–College Retirement Equities Fund)	Leading retirement provider/wealth manager for those in the academic, research, medical, and cultural fields; incorporates ESG principles when appropriate.	$502

Fund Management Companies	Description	Assets Under Management ($ in billions)
Trillium Asset Management	Oldest investment advisor focused exclusively on sustainable and responsible investing; acquired Portfolio21 Global Equity Fund.	$1.7
Turner Investment Partners	Pledged to incorporate ESG considerations into investment decisions.	$4.4
Wellington Management Company, LLP	Integrates ESG standards into investment decisions.	$892

References

Chapter 1. The World on Your Wrist

Bradshaw, Tim, "Apple reports largest profit in history," *The Financial Times*, January 27, 2015. (www.ft.com/intl/cms/s/0/b3bb354a-a666-11e4-89e5-00144feab7de.html#axzz3Q7aHzikH)

Bremmer, Ian, "The New Rules of Globalization," *Harvard Business Review*, January, 2014. (https://hbr.org/2014/01/the-new-rules-of-globalization)

"Collaborative Consumption," *Access*, January, 2015. (http://access.van.fedex.com/collaborative-consumption/)

Crypto-Currency Market Capitalizations. (http://coinmarketcap.com/)

Feloni, Richard, "How Uber CEO Travis Kalanick Went From A Startup Failure To One Of The Hottest Names In Silicon Valley," *Business Insider*, September 24, 2014 (www.businessinsider.com/uber-ceo-travis-kalanicks-success-story-2014-9)

Getlen, Larry, "How the next stage of the Internet's evolution will connect humans and machines," *The New York Post*, March 22, 2015. (http://nypost.com/2015/03/22/how-the-next-stage-of-the-internets-evolution-will-connect-humans-and-machines/?utm_source=Sailthru&utm_medium=email&utm_term=NYP%20180%20Day%20Openers%20and%2030%20Day%20Signups&utm_campaign=NY%2520Post%2520Newsletter)

"Globalization: A Brief Overview," International Monetary Fund. (www.imf.org/external/np/exr/ib/2008/053008.htm)

"Globalization," *Investopedia.* (www.investopedia.com/terms/g/globalization.asp)

Lunden, Ingrid, "Balanced To Close Its Payment Platform, Strikes Transition Deal With Rival Stripe," Telecrunch.com, March 13, 2015. (http://techcrunch.com/2015/03/13/balanced-is-closing-its-marketplace-payment-platform-in-90-days-strikes-transition-deal-with-rival-stripe/)

McLuhan, Marshall, and Quentin Fiore. *War and Peace in the Global Village.* New York: Bantam, 1968.

"Megabytes, Gigabytes, Terabytes . . . What Are They?" (www.whatsa byte.com/)

Mudallal, Zainabl, "Airbnb will soon be booking more rooms than the world's largest hotel chains," *Quartz*, January 20, 2015. (http://qz.com/329735/airbnb-will-soon-be-booking-more-rooms-than-the-worlds-largest-hotel-chains/)

Rogowski, Christina, "The GovLab Index: The Data Universe," The Governance Lab @ NYU, August 22, 2013. (http://thegovlab.org/gov lab-index-the-digital-universe/)

Siegler, MG, "Eric Schmidt: Every 2 Days We Create As Much Information As We Did Up To 2003," TechCrunch.com, August 4, 2010. (http://techcrunch.com/2010/08/04/schmidt-data/)

"The promise of big data," Harvard School of Public Health. (www.hsph.harvard.edu/news/magazine/spr12-big-data-tb-health-costs/)

Chapter 2. The Matter of Energy

"A Comparison: Land Use by Energy Source—Nuclear, Wind and Solar Energy." (www.entergy-arkansas.com/content/news/docs/AR_Nuclear_One_Land_Use.pdf)

Baldwin, Roberto, "Shipshape: Tracking 40 Years of FedEx Tech," *Wired*, April 17, 2013. (www.wired.com/2013/04/40-years-of-fedex/)

Coll, Steve, *Private Empire*. New York: Penguin, 2012, p. 106.

Company Overview, FedEx. (http://investors.fedex.com/company-overview/overview-of-services/default.aspx)

Dumaine, Brian, "Why America's fracking revolution won't be hurt (much) by low oil prices," *Fortune*, December 2, 2014. (http://fortune.com/2014/12/02/why-americas-fracking-revolution-wont-be-hurt-much-by-low-oil-prices/)

"Energy Story," Energy Quest. (www.energyquest.ca.gov/story/chapter 17.html)

"Fossil fuel divestment: a $5 trillion challenge," *Bloomberg New Energy Finance*, August 25, 2014, pp. 4–5, 8.

Gillis, Justin, "Bill Gates and Other Business Leaders Urge U.S. to Increase Energy Research," The New York Times, February 23, 2015. (www.nytimes.com/2015/02/24/us/top-us-business-leaders-urge-increased-energy-research.html?_r=0)

"Gulf Oil Spill," Smithsonian Ocean Portal. (http://ocean.si.edu/gulf-oil-spill)

"How Much Electricity Comes From Renewable Sources," *The New York Times*, March 23, 2013. (www.nytimes.com/interactive/2013/03/24/sunday-review/how-much-electricity-comes-from-renewable-sources.html?ref=sunday-review&_r=0)

Idle, Tom, "What are the 3 mega-trends that could prove the end is in sight for fossil fuels?" Energy & Carbon Management, March 2, 2015. (www.2degreesnetwork.com/groups/2degrees-community/resources/what-3-mega-trends-that-could-prove-end-sight-fossil-fuels/)

"Investors Managing $2.5 Trillion Press Energy Companies to Better Disclose Spill Prevention and Response Plans For Deepwater Wells Worldwide," PR Newswire. (www.prnewswire.com/news-releases/investors-managing-25-trillion-press-energy-companies-to-better-disclose-spill-prevention-and-response-plans-for-deepwater-wells-worldwide-100033799.html)

Let Us Connect Your Supply Chain Globally, FedEx. (http://ftn.fedex.com/us/)

"Oil can do more," Wintershall. (www.wintershall.com/en/company/oil-and-gas/oil-can-do-more.html)

Popli, Sahil, Peter Rodgers, and Valerie Eveloy, "Trigeneration scheme for energy efficiency enhancement in a natural gas processing plant through turbine exhaust gas waste heat utilization," ScienceDirect, May, 2012. (www.sciencedirect.com/science/article/pii/S0306261911 007355)

Randall, Tom, "Oil's Future Draws Blood and Gore in Investment Portfolios," *The Grid*, November 18, 2013. (www.bloomberg.com/ news/2013-11-18/oil-s-future-draws-blood-and-gore-in-investment-portfolios.html)

Smith, Grant, "How OPEC Weaponized the Price of Oil Against U.S. Drillers," Bloomberg.com, January 9, 2013 (www.bloomberg.com/ news/2015-01-09/why-opec-is-talking-oil-down-not-up-after-48-sell off.html)

"Standards of Business Conduct," ExxonMobil, November, 2011, p. 13.

"Statoil's position on carbon asset risk," Statoil. (www.statoil.com/en/ NewsAndMedia/News/Pages/2013_25Nov_Carbon_asset_risk.aspx)

"Tailings Reduction Technology," COSIA. (www.cosia.ca/tailings-reduction-technology)

Thomas, Rob, "The Logic of Divestment: Why We Have to Kiss Off Big Carbon Now," Social(k), January 27, 2015. (https://socialk.com/blog/ the-logic-of-divestment-why-we-have-to-kiss-off-big-carbon-now/)

"25 Years of Impact," Ceres. (www.ceres.org/about-us/our-history)

Wallace, Bruce, "Most Americans see combating climate change as a moral duty," Reuters, February 27, 2015. (www.reuters.com/article/ 2015/02/27/us-usa-climate-poll-idUSKBN0LV0CV20150227)

"Wapisiw Lookout Reclamation," Suncor. (www.suncor.com/en/ responsible/3708.aspx)

"What is CTI?" Carbon Tracker Initiative. (www.carbontracker.org/)

"Who We Are," Ceres. (www.ceres.org/about-us/who-we-are)

Chapter 3. A Merger of Metrics

"AGR Risk List Q1 Update," GMI Ratings, April 15, 2014. (http:// www3.gmiratings.com/home/2014/04/agr-risk-50-list-q1-update/)

"BCAUSE Impact Report, 2013 Update," Bloomberg, p. 9. (www. bloomberg.com/bcause/content/themes/sustainability-2014/report/ BloombergSustReport2013.pdf)

"Behavioral ESG: Focusing on What Matters," GMI Ratings, August, 2012. (http://www3.gmiratings.com/home/2012/08/behavioral-esg-focusing-on-what-matters/)

Deming, W. Edwards, *Out of Crisis.* Cambridge, MA: The MIT Press, 2000, pp. 23–24.

"Environmental, Social and Governance (ESG) Criteria," Investopedia. (www.investopedia.com/terms/e/environmental-social-and-governance-esg-criteria.asp)

"Environmental, Social and Governance Performance," Thomson Reuters. (http://thomsonreuters.com/about-us/corporate-responsibility/ esg-performance/)

Glac, Katherina, "The Influence of Shareholders on Corporate Social Responsibility: History of Corporate Responsibility Project," Center for Ethical Business Cultures, September 2014, pp 8–9.

"GMI Ratings' 2013 CEO Pay Survey," GMI Ratings, October 22, 2013. (http://www3.gmiratings.com/home/2013/10/gmi-ratings-2013-ceo-pay-survey/)

"Governance Insight Alert: Lannett Company and 19 additional companies," GMI

Ratings, July 28, 2014. (http://www3.gmiratings.com/home/2014/07/ governance-insight-alert-lannett-company-19-additional-companies/)

"Investors Managing $2.5 Trillion Press Energy Companies to Better Disclose Spill Prevention and Response Plans For Deepwater Wells Worldwide," PRNewswire, August 5, 2010. (www.prnewswire.com/ news-releases/investors-managing-25-trillion-press-energy-companies-to-better-disclose-spill-prevention-and-response-plans-for-deepwater-wells-worldwide-100033799.html)

"Local Citizen: Making Sustainable Progress Possible One Community at a Time," CATERPILLAR, Sustainability Report, p. 5. (www.cater pillar.com/en/company/sustainability/sustainability-report.html)

"Making Sustainable Progress Possible: Built For Transforming Lives," CAT.com. (www.cat.com/en_US/company.html)

"MSCI Completes Acquisition of GMI Ratings," GMIRatings.com. (http://www3.gmiratings.com/)

Smale, Alison, and Claire Cain Miller, "Germany Sets Gender Quota in Boardrooms," The New York Times, March 6, 2015. (www.nytimes.com/2015/03/07/world/europe/german-law-requires-more-women-on-corporate-boards.html)

"The world's largest construction machinery manufacturers in 2014, based on construction equipment sales (in billion U.S. dollars)," The Statistics Portal. (www.statista.com/statistics/280343/leading-construction-machinery-manufacturers-worldwide-based-on-sales/)

Chapter 4. Money Matters

"CDP: Driving Sustainable Economies," Carbon Disclosure Project. (www.pe-international.com/america/company/partnerships/carbon-disclosure-project/)

"Environmental Disclosure Tied to Higher Financial Performance," Environmental Leader, September 23, 2013. (www.environmentalleader.com/2013/09/23/environmental-disclosure-tied-to-higher-financial-performance/)

Greenwald, Christopher, and Marc-Olivier Buffle, "Measuring Intangibles: Robecosam's Corporate Sustainability Methodology," January, 2013. (www.robecosam.com/images/CSA_methodology_us.pdf)

Halbert, Gary D., "Fed's Zero Interest Rate Cost Savers A Trillion Dollars," ProFutures Investments, May 13, 2014. (www.profutures.com/article.php/903/)

Ingraham, Christopher, "This depressing chart shows that the rich aren't just grabbing a bigger slice of the income pie—they're taking all of it," *The Washington Post,* September 25, 2014. (www.washingtonpost.com/blogs/wonkblog/wp/2014/09/25/this-depressing-chart-shows-that-the-rich-arent-just-grabbing-a-bigger-slice-of-the-income-pie-theyre-taking-all-of-it/)

Kadlec, Charles, "Nixon's Colossal Monetary Error: The Verdict 40

Years Later," Forbes.com, August 15, 2011. (www.forbes.com/sites/ charleskadlec/2011/08/15/nixons-colossal-monetary-error-the-verdict-40-years-later/)

Kalafut, Pamela Cohen, and Jonathan Low, "The value creation index: quantifying intangible value," *Strategy* & *Leadership*, Volume 29, Issue 5, pp. 9–15.

"Linking Climate Engagement to Financial Performance: An Investor's Perspective," Sustainable Insight Capital Management, September, 2013. (www.google.com/url?sa=t&rct=j&q=&esrc=s&source=web&cd= 4&ved=0CC4QFjAD&url=http%3A%2F%2Fwww.sicm.com%2Fdocs %2FCDP_SICM_VF_page.pdf&ei=2bp9VMGLKe_GsQSA-4HoDQ &usg=AFQjCNGmuZfZ-hM-pHOn9-eM3NoQhKtf0w&bvm= bv.80642063,d.cWc)

Makower, Joel, "Why sustainability leaders don't impress Wall Street," Greenbiz.com, August 4, 2014. (www.greenbiz.com/blog/2014/08/04/ why-sustainability-leaders-dont-impress-wall-street)

"Our Understanding of Responsibility," Deutsche Bank. (www.db.com/ cr/index_en.htm)

"SASB Releases Provisional Sustainability Accounting Standards for Financials Industries, Second Set of Standards Issued for Use by Companies and Investors," CSRwire, February 25, 2014. (www.csrwire. com/press_releases/36747-SASB-Releases-Provisional-Sustainability-Accounting-Standards-for-Financials-Industries-Second-Set-of-Standards-Issued-for-Use-by-Companies-and-Investors-)

"Standard & Poor's Global Industry Classification Standard." (www. standardandpoors.com/servlet/BlobServer?blobheadername3=MDT-Type&blobcol=urldata&blobtable=MungoBlobs&blobheadervalue2= inline%3B+filename%3DGICS_MAPBOOL_electronic_0711.pdf& blobheadername2=Content-Disposition&blobheadervalue1=application %2Fpdf&blobkey=id&blobheadername1=content-type&blob where=1243945221356&blobheadervalue3=UTF-8)

"Standards Download," Sustainability Accounting Standards Board. (www.sasb.org/standards/download/)

"Timothy Smith," Conference-Board.org. (www.conference-board.org/ bio/index.cfm?bioid=1807)

Worrachate, Anchalee, and David Goodman, "Currency Trading at $5 Trillion a Day Volumes Surpass Pre-Lehman Peak, BIS Estimates," Bloomberg Business, March 12, 2012. (www.bloomberg.com/news/2012-03-11/currency-trading-at-5-trillion-a-day-surpassed-pre-lehman-high-bis-says.html)

Yousuf, Hibah, "Only half of all Americans invested in stocks," CNN Money, May 9, 2013. (http://money.cnn.com/2013/05/09/investing/american-stock-ownership/)

Chapter 5. Social Response Investing

"Alpha from Sustainability," Clean Investor 2011, Responsible Investor, June 30, 2011. (www.responsible-investor.com/images/uploads/reports/Clean_Investor_2011_Report.pdf)

"Company Performance Linked to CSR, Deutsche Bank Finds," Environmental Leader, June 15, 2012. (www.environmentalleader.com/2012/06/15/company-performance-linked-to-csr-deutsche-bank-finds/)

"Corporate Clout 2013: Time for Responsible Capitalism," Global Trends. (www.globaltrends.com/knowledge-center/features/shapers-and-influencers/190-corporate-clout-2013-time-for-responsible-capitalism)

"Deutsche Bank publishes Corporate Responsibility Report 2013," Deutsche Bank Responsibility. (www.db.com/cr/en/concrete-deutsche_bank_publishes_corporate_responsibility_report_2013.htm)

Eccles, Robert G., Ioannis Ioannou, and George Serafeim," "The Impact of a Corporate Sustainability on Organizational Process and Performance," Harvard Business School, November 14, 2011. (http://hbswk.hbs.edu/item/6865.html)

"From SRI to ESG: The Changing World of Responsible Investing," commonfund institute, September, 2013. (www.commonfund.org/InvestorResources/Publications/White%20Papers/Whitepaper_SRI%20to%20ESG%202013%200901.pdf)

Kramer, Michael, "2014: The year sustainable investment went mainstream," GreenBiz, December 29, 2014 (www.greenbiz.com/article/2014-year-sustainable-investment-went-mainstream?mkt_tok=3RkM

MJWWfF9wsRogv6TAZKXonjHpfsX56%2BUoXaC%2BlMI%2F0E
R3fOvrPUfGjI4HSMVgI%2BSLDwEYGJlv6SgFSLHEMa5qw7gM
XRQ%3D)

Report On US Sustainable, Responsible and Impact Investing Trends
2014," The Forum for Sustainable and Responsible Investment. (www.
google.com/url?sa=t&rct=j&q=&esrc=s&source=web&cd=2&ved=0C
CkQFjAB&url=http%3A%2F%2Fwww.ussif.org%2FFiles%2FPubli-
cations%2FSIF_Trends_14.F.ES.pdf&ei=30mcVNq6MIL7gwSKzoD
YAg&usg=AFQjCNGgtZ9e9Bb2dGOKBm2BtYuHpivmqA&sig2=08j
BbVFFWwD34mJE9c9DJw)

"Signatories to the Principles for Responsible Investment," UNPRI.
org. (www.unpri.org/signatories/signatories/)

"Towards Sustainable Investment: Taking Responsibility," CalPERS.
(www.calpers.ca.gov/docs/forms-publications/esg-report-2012.pdf)

2005 Report on Socially Responsible Investing Trends in the United
States," Social Investment Forum, January 24, 2006. (www.google.com/
url?sa=t&rct=j&q=&esrc=s&source=web&cd=3&ved=0CCoQFjAC&
url=http%3A%2F%2Fwww.ussif.org%2Ffiles%2FPublications%2F05
_Trends_Report.pdf&ei=LlmlVJrlBombNqCCgfAD&usg=AFQjC
NEyIAG34pI1C0Jl_6ZmvPZBwjpzUQ&sig2=GIyh7qBKS-3ORTRB
nSqp8g&bvm=bv.82001339,d.eXY)

Weber, Olaf, Marco Mansfeld, and Eric Schirrmann," The Financial
Performance of SRI Funds Between 2002 and 2009," Social Science
Research Network, June 25, 2010. (http://papers.ssrn.com/sol3/papers.
cfm?abstract_id=1630502)

White, Amanda, "Young ESG veteran sees move to mainstream,"
top1000funds.com, August 10, 2011. (www.top1000funds.com/news/
2011/08/10/young-esg-veteran-sees-move-to-mainstream/)

Chapter 6. Engines of Freedom

American Public Transportation Association, *2008 Public Transportation
Fact Book*, 59th ed, June, 2008. (www.apta.com/resources/statistics/
Documents/FactBook/APTA_2008_Fact_Book.pdf)

"Catalytic Converters," *Environpedia*. (www.enviropedia.org.uk/Air_
Quality/Catalytic_Converters.php)

"China imposes strict fuel economy standards on auto industry," Reuters, March 20, 2013. (www.reuters.com/article/2013/03/20/china-auto-fuel-idUSL3N0CC2EK20130320)

LeBeau, Phil, "Global auto sales hit record high of 82.8 million," CNBC.com, January 9, 2014. (www.cnbc.com/id/101321938#)

"Negative Impact of the Automobile," Colorado.edu. (http://l3d.cs.colorado.edu/systems/agentsheets/New-Vista/automobile/negative.html)

"Number of Cars Worldwide Surpasses 1 Billion; Can the World Handle this Many Wheels?" *The Huffington Post*, August 23, 2011. (www.huffingtonpost.ca/2011/08/23/car-population_n_934291.html)

About the Author

Bruce Piasecki is the president and founder of AHC Group, Inc., a management consulting firm specializing in energy, materials, and environmental corporate matters. His firm's clients include international companies, as well as a distinct set of leaders in business and society that meet with his team twice a year in a membership-driven Corporate Affiliates Program. Since 1981, he has advised over forty-eight of the Fortune 500 on the critical areas of corporate governance, energy, climate change, environmental strategy, product innovation, and sustainability. He served on Vice President Al Gore's White House Council on Environmental Technology, and was assigned a post under Governor Mario Cuomo as an advisor/researcher for New York State Energy Research and Development.

Dr. Piasecki received his master's degree and doctorate from Cornell University. He was a tenured professor at both Clarkson University and the business school at Rensselaer Polytechnic Institute in Troy, New York. While teaching at Clarkson, he founded the AHC Group in 1981. Dr. Piasecki is the author of ten other books on business strategy, valuation, and corporate change, including the *New York Times* bestseller *Doing More With Less*.

A highly sought-after speaker and educator, Dr. Piasecki offers lectures, workshops, and seminars throughout North America and the world. For more information regarding the author, visit his website at www.brucepiasecki.com.

Index

DOING MORE WITH LESS

The New Way to Wealth

Bruce Piasecki

Benjamin Franklin knew instinctively what so many of us have forgotten: Frugality and industriousness are the ways to wealth. Today, many powerful interests, from governments to multinational corporations, are exploring this path and discovering how doing more with less can help secure their future.

Doing More With Less dives into our primal competitive instinct, embracing frugality as a crucial competitive edge. Providing relevant examples from his more than thirty years as a management consultant and change agent, author Bruce Piasecki convincingly explains the case for a return to frugality. Liberate more of your resources by realigning money, people, and rules in your life that impact your family and your company. This book is an actionable call to arms, with global insights—applicable to professionals in any industry—that will make you more adept in the short run and adaptive in the long run.

Through frugality, we recognize obligations beyond our own needs and capture greater returns for ourselves, our families, and our firms. Let "doing more with less is success" be your mantra.

$16.95 US • 208 pages • 6 x 9-inch quality paperback • ISBN 978-0-7570-0426-1

DOING MORE WITH TEAMS

The New Way to Winning

Bruce Piasecki

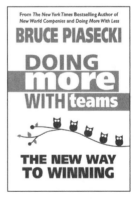

Since the "hunter-gatherer" days of old, human beings have instinctively worked in teams. But what have we really learned about what drives us to cooperate and collaborate with each other? Does all of the selfishness and scandal in business and government today suggest we have spilled the special sauce of teamwork?

Doing More With Teams explores the ways to encourage a new form of competition so that organizations complete the challenges before them to drive growth and get results. It offers a new premise for the concept of teamwork and challenges the perception that individualism is the only way to wealth. Through real-life and historical examples of teams that have inspired awe, this book lays out a solid set of principles that work for all kinds of teams. It shows how to avoid individual motivators that undermine the importance of teams, how to establish guidelines for shared responsibilities, and so much more.

Doing More With Teams enlightens the world to a new, more ethical and more collaborative way forward. It shows us how best to tap into the magic of teamwork.

$16.95 US • 192 pages • 6 x 9-inch quality paperback • ISBN 978-0-7570-0427-8

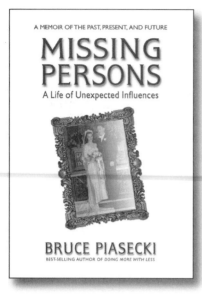

A MEMOIR OF THE PAST, PRESENT, AND FUTURE

MISSING PERSONS

A Life of Unexpected Influences

BRUCE PIASECKI
BEST-SELLING AUTHOR OF *DOING MORE WITH LESS*

MISSING PERSONS
A Life of Unexpected Influences
Bruce Piasecki

After losing his father at age three, noted business entrepreneur Bruce Piasecki was raised by a loving mother who took in foster children to make ends meet. Although his was a childhood fraught with formidable challenges and much sacrifice, Bruce managed to rise above the fray and become a successful voice in the world of business. As president and founder of AHC Group, Inc., he has served as an adviser to dozens of Fortune 500 companies, and his seminal books on business policy include *New York Times* bestseller *Doing More With Less: The New Way to Wealth.*

In *Missing Persons: A Life of Unexpected Influences,* Piasecki celebrates the people and the events that have helped shape—and continue to shape—the person he has become. Through a series of masterfully written vignettes that are part autobiographical and part creative nonfiction, he brings his memoir to life in three parts—his youth, his middle years, and his yet-to-be-lived future. Throughout, you will come to know his mother, his father, his foster brothers and sisters, his wife, his daughter, and the many muses who have touched both his body and soul. Piasecki tells his story in a unique third-person narrative that provides intrigue and drama for readers as they follow him through loss, passion, self-invention, and a litany of fears and dreams, each revealed in eloquent prose.

Compelling and life-affirming, *Missing Persons* helps us to understand the powerful influence of memory, while providing an opportunity to pause, reflect, and recount the myriad of influences in our own lives.

$17.95 US • 224 pages • 6 x 9-inch quality paperback • ISBN 978-0-7570-0412-4

THE NEW ART OF NEGOTIATING
How to Close Any Deal

Gerard I. Nierenberg and Henry H. Calero

You negotiate every day of your life.
Whether you are closing a business
deal, asking your employer for a raise,
or persuading your child to do his
homework, everything is a negotiation.
Written by Gerard Nierenberg and
Henry Calero, world-renowned experts
in the field, *The New Art of Negotiating*
introduces you to the many crucial
skills involved in effective negotiation.

Early in their careers, Nierenberg and Calero came to an important
realization: Negotiation does not have to be an adversarial process that
ends in victory for one party and defeat for the other. By having a clear
understanding of each party's goals, you can steer clear of the common
obstacles that derail most deals. *The New Art of Negotiating* provides
the authors' proven strategies for avoiding these pitfalls in our fast-
changing, high-pressured world. You will learn how to analyze your
opponent's motivation, negotiate toward mutually satisfying terms,
learn from your opponent's body language, and much more.
Throughout, the authors will guide you in successfully applying
their famous "everybody wins" tactics.

Gerard Nierenberg and Henry Calero have changed the way we think
about negotiating, elevating the process to an exciting new level.
With *The New Art of Negotiating,* you can control your own destiny
and experience win-win success in today's challenging business and
social climate.

$15.95 US • 208 pages • 6 x 9-inch quality paperback • ISBN 978-0-7570-0305-9

THE STREET SMART SALES PRO
How to Create, Influence, and Close Any Sale
Arthur Rogen

Evaluate the top producers in any sales force, and you'll find salespeople who are positive, aggressive, and motivated; people who are confident and think quickly on their feet; people who know how to get things done; people who are just plain street smart. They learned their skills from doing, asking, and observing. And now, thanks to *The Street Smart Sales Pro,* these valuable lessons are available to those looking to supercharge their own ability to sell.

The Street Smart Sales Pro offers a realistic "street smart" point of view, focusing on real people in real situations. It covers every aspect of selling, from highlighting the essential qualities that make up the truly triumphant salesperson, to providing hundreds of practical tips, insights, and tactics needed to make that initial contact and successfully close the deal.

No matter how difficult the challenge ahead or how many doors have been closed to you in the past, knowing how to be a street smart sales pro will allow you to see the world as a place filled with opportunities. Ready to boost your sales savvy? There's no better teacher than *The Street Smart Sales Pro.*

$16.95 US • 224 pages • 6 x 9-inch quality paperback • ISBN 978-0-7570-0390-5

HOW TO READ A PERSON LIKE A BOOK
Observing Body Language to Know
What People Are Thinking
Gerard I. Nierenberg, Henry H. Calero, and Gabriel Grayson

Imagine meeting someone for the first time and within minutes—without a word being said—having the ability to tell what that person is thinking. Magic? Not quite. Whether people are aware of it or not, their body movements clearly express their attitudes and motives, communicating key information that is invaluable in a range of situations.

How to Read a Person Like a Book will teach you how to interpret the nonverbal signals of business associates, friends, loved ones, and even strangers. Best-selling authors Nierenberg, Calero, and Grayson have put their working knowledge of body language into this practical guide to recognizing and understanding body movements. They share their proven techniques for detecting lies, gaining control of negotiations, and even recognizing signs of sexual attraction. You will discover how reading body language is a unique skill that offers real and important benefits.

$13.95 US • 128 pages • 6 x 9-inch quality paperback • ISBN 978-0-7570-0314-1

How to Start a Business & Ignite Your Life

A Simple Guide to Combining Business Wisdom with Passion

Ernesto Sirolli, PhD

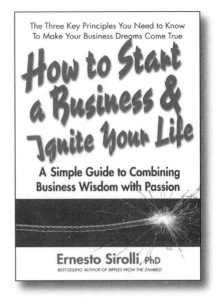

Have you ever wondered why such companies as Apple, Disney, eBay, and Starbucks succeeded? What common factors did they—and most other successful startups—share? Dr. Ernesto Sirolli, one of the world's leading consultants on the topic of economic development, has the answer: None of the entrepreneurs who founded the world's greatest companies did it on their own. They put together an effective team that allowed their ventures to get off the ground, flourish, and grow. And in his new book, *How to Start a Business & Ignite Your Life,* Ernesto Sirolli has written down an easy-to-follow formula for success so that passionate people can transform their ideas into thriving businesses.

Ernesto Sirolli's approach to entrepreneurship is guided by the Trinity of Management, a business model/philosophy based on the idea that there are three key areas in all companies—product, marketing, and financial management. A business has the greatest chance of achieving long-term success when there is a team with the talent and knowledge needed to manage each area effectively. The first half of the book provides an overview of this concept before delving more deeply into the three areas, highlighting various personality traits and skills required for each role. In the second half, Dr. Sirolli explains how these ideas can be practically applied to your startup, enabling you to turn it into a prosperous enterprise.

Whether you are an aspiring entrepreneur or a current business owner looking to revitalize your company, *How to Start a Business & Ignite Your Life* will give you the tools you need to make a living by doing what you love.

$14.95 US • 144 pages • 6 x 9-inch quality paperback • ISBN 978-0-7570-0374-5

AHC Group's Corporate Affiliate Program

Join the discussion along with our other members including:

The AHC Group is a management consulting firm specializing in critical areas of corporate governance, sustainability, energy, product, and environmental strategy.

Our best practices workshops have provided access to a premiere network of leaders from hundreds of the best global firms for more than thirty years.

Members benefit from engaging in provocative and innovative discussion of the world's current and emerging critical business and social issues.

To learn more about what we do, visit our website at
www.ahcgroup.com